MARY
as You've Never
Seen Her Before

MARY
as You've Never Seen Her Before

A Woman from Scripture

Anne SOUPA
Sylvaine LANDRIVON

Paulist Press
New York / Mahwah, NJ

Scripture quotations are from New Revised Standard Version Bible: Catholic Edition, copyright © 1989, 1993 National Council of the Churches of Christ in the United States of America. Used by permission. All rights reserved worldwide.

Cover image: *Madonna and Child*. 1488. Giovanni Bellini.
Cover and book design by Lynn Else

Originally published as *Marie telle que vous ne l'avez jamais vue* by Salvator Editions, Paris, 2024, YVES BRIEND ÉDITEUR (S.A.).

Library of Congress Cataloging-in-Publication Data
Names: Soupa, Anne author | Landrivon, Sylvaine, 1956- author
Title: Mary as you've never seen her before: a woman from scripture / Anne Soupa, Sylvaine Landrivon.
Description: Paperback. | New York; Mahwah, NJ : Paulist Press, [2026] | Includes bibliographical references. | Summary: "This book deconstructs the image of Mary, mother of Jesus, as she has been portrayed through the centuries and constructs a new portrait of Mary based on the careful examination of Scripture"—Provided by publisher.
Identifiers: LCCN 2025037299 (print) | LCCN 2025037300 (ebook) | ISBN 9780809157990 paperback | ISBN 9780809189656 ebook
Subjects: LCSH: Mary, Blessed Virgin, Saint—History of doctrines | Mary, Blessed Virgin, Saint—Biblical teaching | Bible—Criticism, interpretation, etc. | Catholic church—Doctrines
Classification: LCC BT610 .S658 2026 (print) | LCC BT610 (ebook)
LC record available at https://lccn.loc.gov/2025037299
LC ebook record available at https://lccn.loc.gov/2025037300

ISBN 978-0-8091-5799-0 (paperback)
ISBN 978-0-8091-8965-6 (ebook)

Published by Paulist Press
997 Macarthur Boulevard
Mahwah, NJ 07430
www.paulistpress.com

Printed and bound in the
United States of America

To Marie C.
ray of light, dear to our heart

CONTENTS

PREFACE

BEFORE BEING WRITTEN, these pages already had a history, that of an "adventure 2.0" experienced during the lockdown of 2020. Long-time followers of theological explorations and the commitments to which they lead, in particular concerning women in the Catholic Church, the two of us—Sylvaine and Anne—felt the need for a strong and, above all, nourishing message that could reach our then-confined sisters and brothers who, due to their imposed isolation, were almost mesmerized by their television or computer screens. Video conferences offered our open minds opportunities to see, experience, and think in a refreshing way. When the mind is freer, it flushes out certain preconceived ideas, weighs the accuracy of their content, illuminates them with new elements, and finally it strengthens each person's free will. In short, confinement proved to be a fruitful time to revisit the old in order to find something new.

For us Catholics, women caught in the masculine predisposition of our Church, how better to undertake this project than by looking closely at the greatest female figure in Christianity, Mary, the mother of Jesus?

We already guessed that this work would allow us better to understand the weight of male domination over women. And in fact, in the abundance of speeches, dogmatic statements, and gestures of piety toward Mary, the incredible control of the Church over women's bodies, over their words, and over the places to which it assigned their existence, was revealed in broad daylight. No biblical figure has been sacrificed to male domination as much as Mary.

By making this choice, we knew that we were going to tackle the Mount Everest of the Catholic world, because Mary has a very elevated position in the Church and even in civil society. Would the mobilization around restoring the burnt Notre-Dame de Paris have been as strong if the cathedral had borne the name of another saint? Mary belongs to our common heritage. She is a jewel of Catholicism because she softens the tragic life of Jesus and the radical nature of his message with a maternal, familiar, tender, and benevolent figure. When the image of a severe God the Father was imposed, she helped to soften it. Not all religions are fortunate enough to be able to use the face of a young woman holding a child on her knees. An image of simple happiness, a joyful contemplation of life that gives itself and grows, capable of both bringing its spectators back to the lost paradise of a carefree childhood and directing them toward the future. This "Mary and child" populates churches and adorns homes; she has inspired infinite works of art, some of unmatched heights.

But that is not all. Mary also shoulders the worst tragedy of existence. In the extreme solitude that envelops those who lose a child, in their inability to express their pain, Mary offers her example: she, at least, understands without long speeches, because she has been there. These characteristics make Mary a figure of powerful attraction. But they also make any modification of the icon that has been constructed very difficult. Who can fight against this "Mary as the public wants to see her"? Who can try to change or even to modify these features that long Christian practice has constructed? No one can risk it without delicacy and respect. For our part, we will try to do this by reaffirming our pride in counting Mary as one of our treasures. It is because we are attached to Mary that we want to give her back the colors that the Gospels gave her. If we begin our journey with a period of deconstruction, it is because history has dimmed these colors, and we are all currently deprived of them.

In the Christian world, despite very ancient prayers, many devotions, and many pilgrimages with Mary as their object, some people are moving away from the tender image that we have just described. Instead of seeing in Mary the model of what is experienced every day in millions of homes in which a mother takes care of her child and nurtures the child toward fulfillment, some have convinced themselves that she was a figure who deviated from the laws of common humanity. Here and there, Mary began to appear to the smallest of the faithful, the poor or children, to deliver enigmatic messages that are tirelessly commented on. Moreover, Marian vocabulary has seen an excessive increase in emphatic exaggerated titles: "beauty with resplendent force," "queen of heaven," "star of the sea." To accommodate all these exceptional qualifiers, Mary has become an extraordinary woman, inaccessible and compelling. Several times throughout history, quite powerful Catholic currents have even wanted to divinize her, sometimes speaking of her as if, with the Father, the Son, and the Holy Spirit, she had become the fourth person of the Trinity.

But, like any excess, these praises have given rise to reframing. In the sixteenth century, Luther vigorously contested the excesses of the cults of the saints, especially those of Mary. And in the Catholic Church, the Second Vatican Council (1962–1965) brought Catholics back to greater restraint.

It is also necessary to integrate a major fact into the Marian nebula. Mary is a political figure. The relative lack of information that the scriptures provide has allowed the institution to speak in her place by filling the silences in the texts or interpreting them according to its directives. As a squatter occupies an empty dwelling, the Church has invested Mary with the political message that it wanted to convey concerning women. But this message, perhaps still audible yesterday, has become unbearable to women today. It has generated a powerful movement of rejection. How could an emancipated woman accept being reduced to the submission to which the manipulated figure of Mary confines her? How many women have therefore quietly left a Church that understands them so poorly? But in this little game, everyone loses. By reducing Mary to the rank of a doll that clerical actors make speak on command when it suits them, the institution discredits itself, and all Catholics deprive themselves of the most beautiful illustration of dynamic faith.

At the start of our work, we realized how complicated the relationship with Mary is, as much for each Catholic as for the Church. Her figure is divisive, between passion and reason, between excess and rejection, between official discourse and exegetical truth. On the one hand, the emotional attachments to Mary are multiple and respectable; they offer an effective opportunity to express one's feelings and better understand the issues of faith that Mary experienced. But they must not rely on the texts without analyzing them. On the other hand, the institutional hold on Mary is so omnipresent, even if it is little admitted, that the biblical truth struggles to appear.

We have both gone through these observations from the inside, not only through our work on the subject, but also through our involvement in the life of the Church. We have both approached Marian piety, either our own or that of our loved ones, then we have questioned the presuppositions of the commentators and, as honestly as possible, we have rejected those which contradicted the scriptures, with the help of recent exegetical studies. Through patient investigation, we have combined our two voices, our knowledge, and our sensibilities.

Little by little, from under clerical rewritings and the dressings of devotion, another Mary has revealed herself. She has surprised us and pushed us to admiration. Mary, we can now state without hesitation, is a powerful, rich, complex figure; she has the strength of the prophets and an incredible vigor. We have encountered a "Mary as we have never seen her before," who meets contemporary expectations and nourishes faith.

In many respects, the story of the young woman who lived in the first century will remain unavailable because the evangelists do not present a historical chronicle in the modern sense of the word but offer an "edifying story" that builds faith.

In our exploration, we have sometimes allowed ourselves parallels and consonances from one Gospel to another. In this way, we hope to have better highlighted Mary's overall contribution to the fulfillment of the scriptures in line with what Jesus announces.

Mary of the Gospels—bold, a feminist before her time—this Mary awaits us at the end of the journey.

INTRODUCTION

THE TITLE GIVEN to our project clearly indicates its ambition—deconstructing in order to rebuild. Over the centuries, the accumulation of emotional impulses and political machinations around the mother of Jesus ended up crushing the message from the Gospels. And, over the course of these shifts, the faith of Catholics gradually adapted to an image of Mary remodeled by men to serve other purposes than that with which the Gospel had invested it.

Let us begin with the emotional impulses of the faithful. First, we must remember that, in the unfolding of sacred history, Mary is an exceptional figure. To whom could we compare her? To no one, because she is the mother of the Lord and therefore unique. And, to state the obvious, being a mother, she is a woman. These two characteristics carry two major risks. The first is to allow the most powerful identification in the West, that of the reader with "the mother," a mother who, moreover, is overcome by the worst of sufferings, that of the death of a child. What mother could not, quite legitimately, see herself close to such a figure, to the point of praying to her, of confiding her sorrows and doubts to her, of hoping for her intercession?

Another truism is that all human beings are sons and daughters, and if they display their predilection for Mary, it is perhaps because they transfer to her their original ties with their mother. This eventuality has serious consequences for sons who, in their early childhood, must separate themselves from a certain maternal image. Thus, in Catholicism, where priests are celibate, it may be that no female figure has come to dethrone the mother. In their unconscious mind, the mother remains omnipresent. Isn't she sometimes too much?

This psychological reference is inevitable, because our feelings precede our thoughts, even if we try to make them rational. It is also legitimate, because its harmonics create links between our humanity and that of Mary, capable of helping us to heal sadness or resolve internal conflicts. But it must neither betray the biblical image nor replace it. Even if it is a demanding ethic and probably never completely successful, we do not have to project our moods or our cultural identifications onto a figure that transmits infinitely more than what we try to enclose it in. Because in doing so, we limit its scope for ourselves, and we impose our images on others. From then on, unconsciously or deliberately, this displacement becomes a lie. If it is an institution that leads this distortion, it is at fault.

The second risk is that of manipulating Mary for political ends, making her the woman par excellence, particularly docile to the male domination in force in the Catholic Church. Returning to scripture, we will show that this model of "a woman" who would be emblematic of all women has been largely imposed, not only in ancient centuries, but also in recent decades by recent popes. Yet we must affirm that if women recognize themselves in Mary, men can do so just as well. The great spiritual figures of the Middle Ages, such as Saint Bernard of Clairvaux, often relied on the figure of Mary to show that the believer symbolically gave birth to Christ. It is therefore important to correct the schema according to which Mary would embody "the woman"; the one who, by her "obedience," would repair the "fault" of Eve. In reality, there are only "women" with plural trajectories, irreducible to a single model. We must therefore deconstruct these deviant teachings, because they are traps for the growth of humanity. To free Mary from the caricatures and biases that have been instrumentalized does not make her lose her strength and splendor. On the contrary, Mary surprises, she dares, and she even shakes things up.

Aware of these distorting prisms and carried by the hope of rediscovering the lively freshness of the mother of Jesus, we conducted our investigation in three stages. The deconstruction stage was laborious and demanding in order to explore all the traps and remove the tinsel with which Catholic tradition had covered Mary.

We questioned Mary's virginity very closely. Why did the institution value this virginity so much? Similarly, the motherhood of Mary, which is made her central attribute, held our attention for a long time.

After this critical exploration, we then gathered all the evidence from our investigation.

Finally, bringing these pieces together, we reconstructed then contemplated this new Mary, both the mother of the Son of God and the mother of the man Jesus, who truly invites us to follow her on the paths that lead to her son.

ABBREVIATIONS

EG *Evangelii Gaudium,* On the Joy of the Gospel, Francis, November 24, 2013

HV *Humanae Vitae*, On the Regulation of Birth, Paul VI, July 25, 1968

LG *Lumen Gentium,* Dogmatic Constitution on the Church, Paul VI, November 21, 1964

MD *Mulieris Dignitatem*, On the Dignity and Vocation of Women, John Paul II, August 15, 1988

TOB Traduction œcuménique de la Bible (*Ecumenical Translation of the Bible*)

WORKS BY ANNE SOUPA

Galla Placidia, l'impératrice face aux grandes migrations, Cerf, 2025

Douze femmes dans la vie de Jésus, Salvator, 2025

Pâques. Art du passage, Cerf, 2022

Espérez! Manifeste pour la renaissance du christianisme, with Christine Pedotti, Albin Michel, 2022

Judas. Le coupable idéal, Albin Michel, 2018

Le jour où Luther a dit non, Salvator, 2017

Pour l'amour de Dieu, Albin Michel, 2021

Dieu aime-t-il les femmes?, Médiaspaul, 2012

Consoler les catholiques, Salvator, 2019

Les pieds dans le bénitier, with Christine Pedotti, Presses de la Renaissance, 2011

L'ange de la force au chevet de l'amour, with André Gouzes, Bayard, 2016

François. La divine surprise, Médiaspaul, 2014

Faut-il croire au diable?, with Marie-Michèle Bourrat, Bayard, 1995

WORKS BY SYLVAINE LANDRIVON

En finir avec les idées fausses sur le christianisme, L'Atelier/Temps Présent, 2026

La Part des femmes. Relire la Bible pour repenser l'Église, L'Atelier, 2024

Les Leçons de Béthanie. De la théorie à la pratique, Cerf, 2022

La Voie royale. Vivre l'accouchement comme une Pâque et l'oser sans anesthésie, Cerf, 2020

Marie-Madeleine. La fin de la nuit, Cerf, 2017

Marie de Magdala. Apôtre?, Cerf, 2017

La Femme remodelée. Centrer la grâce d'être femme sur la maternité: choix de Dieu ou des hommes?, Cerf, 2016

Faites-les taire…Judith, un enseignement subversif, Olivétan, 2014

Part 1
DECONSTRUCTION

IN THE PANOPLY of religious sciences, where is Mary? In the "Bible" section, or in the "Church" section? "In the Bible section" would be the spontaneous answer since she appears in all the Gospels. Well, no, Mary has been placed under the "Church" heading. This shift raises questions. It is explained by the fact that the Gospels speak relatively little of Mary, even if she is, of course, present: about ten quotes or stories. For example, she is cited less often than Peter or Mary Magdalene.

But this assignment to the rubric of "Church"—and the assimilation of Mary to the Church herself—has proven to be fraught with consequences, as it has opened the door to unspeakable excesses. Shamelessly ignoring the rigor that should accompany the study of source texts, eager commentators have filled in the blanks in the text with what they wanted to hear. Either they have reinforced the male domination of the time or, more often, they have frolicked in the many twists of their subjectivity and imposed it on the faithful. Because of this, the figure of Mary has become a victim of major distortions compared to the original message of the Gospels, resembling today more a "lobotomized ornament"[1] than the mother of the Savior.

In this critical section of our book, the first chapter will note the deformations that Mary underwent, and the second will recall what popular piety as well as the Church expect from them. We will then question what we understand by "virginity," and then, in a final chapter, we will look at Mary's extraordinary motherhood.

1

A LOBOTOMIZED FIGURE

LET US GO and meet this counterfeit representation. To summarize in a few lines, the Catholic tradition has made Mary a young woman far removed from the pleasures of the flesh, almost "disembodied," silent and obedient, whom adversity transforms into a mother of sorrows. Submissive to everything around her, she acquiesces to the angel with a certain fatalism (as she submits to her mortality). At the foot of the cross, she is given another son in the person of the beloved disciple, then she leaves this world in a way as evanescent as it is miraculous.

If we look at how the figure of Mary was constructed, we observe that it is based on two presuppositions: Mary as the antithesis of Eve, the mother of the origins of history, and Mary as the model of every woman.

DISOBEDIENT EVE AND SUBMISSIVE MARY

The approach of the first fathers of the Church was to compare Mary to Eve in order better to distinguish her. Let us follow the same path, go back in time, and ask ourselves, why did the early fathers have to seize upon the figure of Eve, "the mother of all who live" (Gen 3:20), to contrast her with Mary? In fact, they first needed to scrutinize the scriptures. They sought backing, an announcement, "prophecies," and supports for similarity or opposition. Eve was a figure on which they could not fail to dwell if they understood the function of Mary in the history of salvation. It is precisely there, in this comparison that has been pushed to the point of caricature, that a good part of the fallacious interpretations of Mary that we have inherited originate. Let us therefore accept this detour via the figure of Eve.

First, we must recall the context in which these authors wrote. In the generations that followed Jesus, the leaders of the young Christian communities needed to return to the normality of social relations that Jesus and Paul had somewhat disrupted. Jesus, on the one hand, took a perfectly egalitarian view of men and women, and Paul, on the other hand, affirming that in Christ "there is no longer Jew or Greek, there is no longer slave or free; there is no longer male and female" (Gal 3:28), surrounded himself with collaborators, both male and female. But, at the turn of the second and third centuries, the young Church allowed itself to be caught up in the patriarchal model of the priests of the First Testament. Seeking to institutionalize itself, it chose a religious structure that made room for the "sacred" and restored a distance between the people and God through a body of intermediaries, the priests, who would be chosen only from among men. It had to provide itself with a feminine figure that illustrated withdrawal and obedience, without being a feminine power capable of rivaling the power of men. This would be Mary, reconstructed by opposing her to the original figure of scripture, Eve.

However, any comparison runs the risk of selecting the features that bring two entities together or separate them, to the detriment of an overall view. The parallel between Eve and Mary, initiated by Saint Irenaeus in the second century, has hardened over time, pushing the initial idea to the point of caricature and misinterpretation. Thus, by wanting to oppose Eve to Mary, we have reduced the richness of both. But if we look at each of them for themselves, then the discoveries are significant, as much for Eve as for Mary.

Eve is a complex figure. Her many facets are still barely sketched by exegetes, and the analyses are difficult and sometimes hazardous. Let us briefly recall her story. In chapter 2 of the Book of Genesis, in the garden of Eden, the human being named by the generic term of *ha adam* and therefore still undifferentiated between "man" and "woman," receives from the Creator a "prohibition," that of eating, under penalty of death, from the tree of the knowledge of good and evil. But, in the following chapter, the couple, now differentiated, is confronted with the serpent. Faced with his insistent words and seeing that the fruit of this tree is good to eat, the woman eats a piece of fruit and gives some to the (male) man. By personalized "judgments," the Creator curses the serpent, multiplies the pains of the woman's pregnancies, curses the ground on which the man must toil, and chases the couple from paradise. For being the first to eat the fruit, Eve was considered by Christian commentators to be responsible for the disobedience, quickly labelled the "fall."

It is essential to identify this term, because it is on this notion of fall or "fault" that the whole framework of what theologians call "redemption" is built. This explains that the Son of God came to earth "to redeem the original sin of the couple." "O truly necessary sin of Adam,"[2] proclaims the Exsultet sung at Easter, "that earned so great, so glorious a Redeemer." And in this context we find a rare occurrence; the sin is attributed to Adam, therefore to the man as much as to the woman. However, none of the words *fall*, *fault*, *salvation*, or *redemption* appears in the biblical text. And we will soon see that nothing overwhelms Eve. It is essential to remember this, especially when we know how much the strong symbolic value of the origin stories makes them an insurmountable norm. Here, instead of encouraging a surge toward life, they have been tasked with telling the indelible downfall brought upon the couple. The dynamics of life have been seriously undermined. In its place, throughout history, guilt has flourished among believers, fueled by what historian Jean Delumeau called "the pastoral of fear," which has been deployed at the expense of the weakest elements of Western societies: women. In fact, this shame that weighs heavily on the couple will strike Eve most of all, and therefore all women after her.

Faced with a disobedient Eve, Mary, who says to the angel Gabriel, "Let it be with me according to your word" (Luke 1:38), offers the diametrically direct opposite in the register of obedience.

According to a formula of Saint Irenaeus that has become popular, Mary is "the new Eve." He explains it with this lapidary phrase: "The knot of Eve's disobedience was undone by Mary's obedience."[3] If Christ is the "new Adam" who saves humanity fallen by sin, Mary is the new Eve who gives birth to the Savior. She becomes the antithetical figure of Eve.

The arrow is fired, ladies; we are targeted! Let us first be surprised that the parallel is not drawn between the two couples, that of the origin story and that of Mary and Joseph, but on the two female figures alone. Let us then recall that this track of "Mary as the new Eve," explored by Saint Irenaeus and his successors, must be handled with caution, in order to avoid the caricature that attributes to women the source of sin, which would be repaired in submission to males, and which, consequently, recognizes men in the role of guide to the human community.

For Irenaeus's construction to be admissible, two pitfalls must be avoided: that of unnecessarily maligning the figures of the First Testament, and that of imputing to the masculine and feminine anthropological schemas that nothing in scripture authorizes.

Let us first analyze Eve herself.

THE "FAULT" OF EVE

Let us return to what we know about Eve. Is she as "guilty" as tradition would have us believe? If we return to chapter 3 of Genesis, which depicts the first relationships of our distant relatives, we observe that a strange adventure takes place in paradise. While God has created a world that seems "very good," a grain of sand seems to have slipped into these idyllic mechanisms and, very quickly, everything deteriorates. Questions abound: Is something missing from these two human beings placed face-to-face? Is the relationship between God and them too asymmetrical for harmony to reign? What are their links, and how can we repay God for the immeasurable love that he gives them by placing them in the garden? Why does the woman let herself be tempted by the serpent when she has everything? But this serpent is also a creature of God. Would we not be wrong to attribute all the responsibility to it?

Let us first question God's attitude. A preliminary, and likely, interpretation would be that God, by maintaining silence, consents to this exploration that Eve is carrying out, without it being possible to say whether God approves of it or not. It is also likely that the biblical writers benefited from the multiple experiences of their lives: that of a lost paradise, of an unattainable good, of excess, of the attraction to transgression, of guilt, and a thousand other realities linked to the human condition. Consequently, the focus on an indelible "original sin" caused by Eve's disobedience at the dawn of humanity appears quite quickly as the transposition of our abilities to sometimes do good and sometimes do evil. Also, we are entitled to see in this a form of injunction: "Do not disobey like Eve but imitate Mary in submission and passivity!" So if, as many clerics repeat, Mary must "redeem" some "fault" of Eve, let us observe the scene even more closely and look for what this first woman could have that needed to be redeemed by another.

Barely had the fruit been eaten (see Gen 3:6), the transgression accomplished, when Eve, in the eyes of the man, appeared less an accomplice than a suspect on whom he was quick to shift the blame: "The woman whom you gave to be with me, she gave me fruit from the tree, and I ate" (Gen 3:12). No attempt at dialogue on Adam's part. Why does he address God directly and not the woman? Does she not belong to the same species as him? Has he not understood the importance of the bond that must unite these first human beings? And has he not, too, heard the prohibition? This attitude so resembles a denial of responsibility and an attempt at domination that it would be legitimate to ask whether in doing so, it would not be the man who would be "at fault." If so, who will "redeem" this fault? Would it be the woman?

However, the woman demonstrates the same propensity as the man: If she has shared the fruit, she does not speak to her partner, but to the serpent, then to God.

A little later, the writer emphasizes that it is to the woman and not to the man that God poses the question of responsibility: "What have you done here?" Their posture, their motivation, perhaps, are different. In return, the divine attitude will not be the same, and the sentences that God will promulgate will affect the woman and the man differently. To the woman, the pain of motherhood (see Gen 3:16), to the man, the pain of work in the fields (see Gen 3:17).

But as the biblical scholar Paul Beauchamp[4] points out, the sentence on the woman is not preceded by any motivation recalling her fault, while that of the man is mentioned (see Gen 3:17). Beauchamp also emphasizes, contrary to the common idea, that God's verdict resembles more a blessing than a punishment. Indeed, the use of the verb "I will multiply" belongs to the formulas of blessing.[5] Would not the Creator indicate here to women that this very particular moment of childbirth allows them to approach a particular truth? This is why the biblical scholar writes: "It seems that the horizon is broader than simple fertility."[6]

Yet the end of the verse stating the sentences denotes a change of tone: "Your desire shall be for your husband, and he shall rule over you." It could lead us toward a condemnation of the woman. In any case, it anticipates the dangers that the blessing granted places on her. Indeed, God grants Eve, "mother of all the living," the power to bear life, but very quickly, this power will lead her to excess. To understand how far the lust and domination evoked in this verse go, we must travel further into the story, to the moment of the conception of the couple's first child, then the second. Thus, in Genesis 4:1, it is said: "The man knew his wife Eve, and she conceived and bore Cain saying, 'I have produced a man with the help of the Lord.'" I have acquired, *qâniti*, "with the Lord"! It is clear from this exclamation that Eve, now removed from God's gaze and already ready to exploit him, considers herself the sole holder of this power, and that her companion remains totally outside the scope of her concerns. The same scenario unfolds with Abel, with the additional circumstance that Abel is not even mentioned as "son" but only as "brother" of his elder. It will be necessary to wait for the conception of another child, after the murder of Abel by Cain, for Eve to accept the relationship that will allow her to avoid this burst of hubris: "Adam knew his wife again, and she bore a son and named him Seth, for, she said, 'God has appointed for me another child'" (Gen 4:25).

The Lord's contribution is more distant; it is only written: "Adam knew his wife again, and she bore a son." From now on, conception takes into account the presence of a father, a human being equal to the mother in dignity. Eve no longer feels an exclusive and direct connection with God.

EVE, NEITHER CURSED NOR GUILTY

These few observations allow our investigation to take a new turn. We are far from the assumptions of the commentators. We are even at the opposite end of the spectrum. We wanted to question the prejudice of submission of women to men, and we discover that it is the woman who exercises domination, as much toward her husband as toward her son. It is rare that ecclesiastical commentaries acknowledge this trait in verse 16c that deals with it precisely. However, during the millennium preceding the common era, the power of the mother goddesses in the polytheistic religions that Israel encountered every day hovered like a danger above the pen of any biblical writer. Also, when the latter speaks of "lust," he is perfectly aware of a primordial feminine domination that should be minimized. He achieves this by counterbalancing the creative power carried by the feminine with the physical power recognized in the male. But let us strongly reaffirm that there is no question of fault or curse against human beings.

On the contrary, it is ultimately a blessing that will be attributed to Eve, which she will experience through motherhood. In this perspective, it now becomes possible to take a peaceful look at this chapter without seeking there the "fall" that has for so long qualified the disobedience of the couple. But it is not useless to return for a moment to the damage caused to women due to the extreme polarization of the Church on the fall of our original parents, also called "original sin."

Fueled by Saint Augustine (fifth century), the theme of the fall and the need for redemption of humanity found its guilt in the person of Eve much more than in that of her companion. Eve, held to be the instigator of original sin, had to assume the role of principal accused in a trial devoid of scriptural anchorage. After her, all women suffered. The Middle Ages and the Renaissance abound in works in which the serpent possesses the head of a woman. Let us recall *The Temptation of Adam and Eve* from the Brancacci Chapel,[7] which followed from numerous medieval manuscripts. This exacerbation of women's guilt is concomitant with Rome's obligation of priestly celibacy, which dates from the twelfth century, but which took a long time to be respected. Over the generations, it was necessary to persuade priests to avoid, for their salvation, the association of women, these daughters of Eve the temptress, the seductress, the agent of the devil. In this context, we can see how much the conviction that humanity has fallen allows the salvific function of Mary to be amplified. The opposition between Eve and Mary then reaches its height. Eve falls, Mary redeems. But if there is no fall, what will be left to redeem?

If we try to be faithful to the biblical text, we discover, in fact, that a mission is given to Eve, because God, in the choice of the sentence addressed to her, not only does not interrupt the act of creation but, in a certain way, delegates it. Through the generation of the couple's sons, human history unfolds, since Eve will be responsible for carrying out by motherhood this act of creation and for transmitting it to the "sons of the promise." The feminine will thus be situated on the side of "realization" and will be able to symbolize the people of Israel, bearers of the message of hope. In this perspective, a link already appears with the one who will engender the Word of God. It is no longer the opposition but the parallel between Eve and Mary that is revealed. In a certain way, it would thus be better to speak of continuity or amplification of the role of the former in the latter.

But to arrive at this positive reading of what God announces to Eve, one must have already paid close attention to the text before the judgments. With the influence of translations and interpretations, omissions with serious consequences creep in. To bring them to light, it is imperative to return to the Hebrew. Literally, it is written in Genesis 3:15: "This one [Eve/the woman] will crush your head,"[8] which is not equivalent to the translation:

"This one will aim at your head,"[9] nor to the version of the Jerusalem Bible that renders the verse as follows: "I will put enmity between you and the woman, between your lineage and hers. He will crush your head." While the question here is of Eve's intervention, this last interpretation ends up sidelining the woman in favor of the "lineage." No doubt it was intended to insinuate that it would be a descendant of Eve who would defeat the serpent. But the translator overlooks the feminine, both grammatically by writing "he will crush you" and omitting the role of "the woman."

This shift is unfortunate, because without this rigorous work on the words, how can we identify that the first announcement of a victory over evil, in other words, the first good news of salvation, is expressed to Eve? The objective of these accommodations with the text was undoubtedly to inflect it so that it better announces Jesus, the Messiah. But the Book of Genesis does not say that; it announces the triumph over evil through the intervention of a woman. If the victory over evil is achieved by a "woman," we rediscover once again the link between these two women, because it is indeed through a woman, Mary, that the Son of God comes into the world and saves it.

In this point of meeting and coherence between Eve and Mary underlining the reading of Genesis, we note that there is no overvaluation of one gender in relation to the other, certainly not from masculine to feminine. In this foundation story, God accepts all of creation without exposing the slightest gender discrimination.

However, this has not been the case throughout the Catholic tradition, where "the representation of the divine mystery has been molded on the role of the monarch, the absolute sovereign,"[10] the one who is embodied in the Church by men, as Elizabeth Johnson develops. Women are now justified in denouncing the limits of a discourse on God woven solely from masculine terms because it does not express the biblical world in which men and women participate equally in the divine principle. Yet even in the errors of the behaviors attributed to Adam and Eve, no term underlines any subordination, even if, as we have seen, lust and domination are like embers that burn the quality of relationships between human beings.

God Beyond Masculine and Feminine

It is quite common today for women's claims to be based on the gender of God. Since most languages use the masculine as a gender determinant, some Christian commentators have been tempted to make God not only a representative of the masculine gender, but also of the masculine sex. There is no better way to impose male domination. To defend the cause of women today, some feminize God: "God-e."

But what do the scriptures say about it?

It seems that they enjoy confusing the issue, calling God by either gender. For example, in chapter 11 of the Book of Hosea, where love is about to triumph, God says: "How can I abandon you, Ephraim?" with accents of tenderness, compassion, and nurturing attributed to the feminine. But a few verses later, when God holds back God's anger in an authoritarian and "manly" reaction, God seems at first to belong to the masculine gender, only to immediately escape it: "for I am God and not male," says the Hebrew text. At the same time, when God, in Isaiah 49:15, affirms: "Even these may forget [their children], yet I will not forget you," he seems to take on the feminine gender. But he is not, however, described as "mother."

From these examples taken from the First Testament, we must remember that the poetic language of the prophets plays with images but does not allow itself to be confined by them. Similarly, the fact that Jesus was born in a male body does not allow us to say that God expresses Godself in a privileged way in the masculine. Could Jesus be of both sexes at the same time? The answer is that God speaks in every human being according to feminine and masculine harmonics that belong specifically to each human being and not, in a generic and absolute way, to the two genders. But it goes without saying that this understanding disrupts traditional models. The most important thing to remember is that God, "beyond all," infinitely exceeds the criteria of sex or gender that we like to attribute to God.

Such a reading free of institutional constraints will highlight that women, as well as men, are images of God through their own abilities, without there being any need for a divinized model such as a Virgin Mary, having lost all connection with her real humanity, would quickly become.

To reconnect the threads of this development, let us assume that if Mary extends the symbolism of the "mother of the living" represented by Eve, it is in order to fulfill the promise and to cooperate in the blossoming of love.

It is then appropriate to deconstruct other schema that blur our encounter with Mary. One of the most established traditions makes Mary the culmination of the feminine model, which, when examined more closely, turns out to be too judiciously adapted to the desires of patriarchy and much less to what scripture transmits. We therefore denounce a caricatured schema of "the" woman.

MARY, "THE" WOMAN?

After the fallacious teaching of an obedient woman who came to repair the fault of another woman through whom sin entered the world, the model of "a woman"—Mary—emblematic of all women, was instilled, even imposed for centuries.

Let us shake off the weight of too many intellectually dishonest comments that have made, and still make, the apology for what the Marian charism should be: obedience and virginity-motherhood. Every woman has been invited to imitate this model without having to worry about following Christ, a model which would be intended for men.

The Church fathers of the first centuries were not, however, all as imprisoned by this schematic representation as those of the nineteenth and twentieth centuries became in a tragic impoverishment. During this last period, two different types of phenomena influenced the magisterial discourses. The first is that of the Marian apparitions of the nineteenth century, which we will only briefly mention here, and the second, Western female emancipation in the twentieth century. On this last subject, the papal reaction was very vigorous, to the point of imposing a very powerful ideological straitjacket on Catholic opinion. So many commentators, clergy, media, but also women, seduced and admiring, have praised the relevance of the words of Pope John Paul II that, in this chapter devoted to Mary, we must show precisely how this pope relied on her to define "woman." Thus, when the pope speaks of "the 'fullness of grace' granted to the Virgin of Nazareth," he specifies that it is "the fullness of the perfection of what is characteristic of women, of what is feminine. We find ourselves here at the central point, at the foundation of the development of the archetype of the personal dignity of women" (ML 5).

This narrowing, this fundamentalism contrary to the Catholic genius, can only be explained in the light of the central objective of the pope in these matters: to preserve priests, by imposing that only men can access the priestly ministry. How? By attributing and emphasizing a "feminine vocation" that would confine women to the private sphere and that the pope believes he finds in Mary. This explains the untimely use of an essentialist ideology.[11]

Our investigation of the Bible throughout these pages will show us that Mary is not the model of a "woman." She is the model of the lifelong believer, man or woman. Yet this is not the language that the papacy intends to convey, certainly not what John Paul II teaches in his many pronouncements on the subject.

Throughout his pontificate (1978–2005), John Paul II never ceased to attribute to motherhood the force of a destiny, while neither women, nor the magisterium, nor a fortiori the scriptures have claimed to define an eternal masculine. What the pope calls "the vocation of women" has no equivalent on the masculine side; it is an assignment due solely to the beliefs of the pontiff. With a disconcerting insistence, John Paul II focuses his concerns both on the feminine condition and on the role of women within the family.

To make the condition of women understood, he repeatedly focuses his speeches on the "dignity"[12] of *the* woman. This ambiguous term allows for uncontestable baptismal equality while avoiding the question of the immediate equality of rights, postponing it "to heaven." In his Apostolic Letter *Mulieris Dignitatem* 27, this pope reduces the feminine vocation to, according to him, the greatest service that it can render, that of devoting itself to the "domestic Church," that is to say to the transmission of the faith in the home. He confirmed this a few years later in his *Letter to Women.*[13]

But what dignity is in question? As surprising as it may seem, it is not the dignity of belonging to the human species, but that of motherhood inscribed in the female body, as a potentiality, whether or not it is realized, or even sometimes possible. And as Patrick Snyder[14] analyzes, John Paul II's reasoning follows a clear logic: Maintaining first that the person is a body, he inscribes this dignity in a body that encompasses its biological, psychic, and spiritual reality. Consequently, as the woman biologically possesses the capacity to bear children, John Paul II deduces that, by her "nature," her specific vocation is to be a mother. This vocation, attributed ex officio due to the presence of a uterus, directs the woman's entire being, formulates her entire person. It perpetuates Hippocrates's conception: *Tota mulier in utero*, the woman is reduced to her uterus! And the body, not recognized for its other potentialities and particularly denigrated when it comes to pleasure, suddenly becomes the sole maternal body, the sole vector of the destiny of the human person afflicted with two *X* chromosomes.

Certainly, John Paul II recognizes that "we have unfortunately inherited a history of very strong *conditioning* which, at all times and in all places, has made the path of women difficult, caused their dignity to be ignored, distorted their prerogatives, has often marginalized and even reduced it to slavery."[15] And, to "transform the face of the earth," he admits that "in this task, which is essentially a work of culture, both man and woman have had an equal responsibility since the beginning."

JOHN PAUL II: MOTHERHOOD AS DESTINY

However, there is something wrong with this speech. The pope does not clearly name male domination and implies that women are also responsible for their subjugation. In this specific case, shifting part of the responsibility onto women is a dishonest undertaking. "Their most natural relationship," the pope continues, "responding to God's plan, is the unity of the two, that is to say a 'dual unity,' relational, which allows each one to discover the interpersonal and reciprocal relationship as a gift, a source of wealth and responsibility."[16] From this observation, logic would dictate that women be entrusted with positions of responsibility within ecclesiastical institutions, to allow this source of wealth to make the Church prosper. But this is not the case. Returning to his mantra, John Paul II recalls that the role of women must remain confined to the areas he reserves for it: the family sphere, the place par excellence of motherhood, education, care of the sick, or consecrated life.

For John Paul II, who takes up Irenaeus's interpretation of Eve but as it has been distorted over time, women, by biology as much as by psyche, are destined for motherhood. As Patrick Snyder explains, "through the archetype of Mary, the new Eve, he proposes to women to find the path to the original acceptance of their body, of their vocation to motherhood,"[17] as if the first woman, taken from the primordial *ha adam*, had been created for this purpose, as if no woman could be a woman outside of this state. We find here the toxic patriarchal use of the first chapters of Genesis that wants the woman to be a "helper" for the man, whereas, as we will see, it is a question of the help of one toward the other.

The assignment of women to motherhood has opportunely served male careerism, which has been able to take advantage of this relegation of half of humanity to the domestic sphere, to occupy, for its own benefit, all positions of power.

In the Catholic Church, the control over governance was pushed to an excess so contrary to the teaching of the New Testament that it was imperative to justify it by strong magisterial writings, especially in the twentieth century, in the post–Vatican II era, when civil society recognized feminine skills outside the sphere of care and the home. This is what John Paul II worked to do. It is significant that most of his statements on this theme took place in tension with the four major United Nations conferences on women and in particular before the last decisive one in 1995,[18] which he strongly opposed.

To define the role of women in society by praising the "dignity" of women makes them swallow the cup of bitterness. But what honey in his mouth to hide it! The woman, according to the image of the Virgin Mary that the institution proposes, becomes for this pope a "superior" being, of incomparable spiritual richness. Based on the division of roles operated by the theologian Hans Urs von Balthasar, who distinguishes a Marian principle (assigned to the feminine) and a Petrine principle (assigned to the masculine), the pope praises the "specific feminine," recognizing them as "much more than men." The biblical scholar Anne-Marie Pelletier observes that these compliments place women "in such an ideal sphere that they do not have to commit themselves to the management of the present of the institution."[19] "Woman" must therefore not dissipate into contingency. By exalting through motherhood the value of a feminine soul "naturally" turned toward service to others, the pope seduces and cajoles part of his female audience and seeks to make them forget that in all areas, he forces women into complete subjugation to male power, both in private and public life. With him, the confiscation of women's bodies, the taboo against contraception other than "natural," and abortion as an "abomination" are reinforced. Regarding abortion, everything happens as if great and numerous theologians had not sought over the centuries to determine the moment of the animation of the fetus. Is it not known in Vatican circles that for William of Conches in the twelfth century, the soul only entered the body at the moment when the conditions necessary for life were fulfilled? Which means, according to these criteria, that an early abortion would not kill a human being and would leave open the possibility of respecting women's bodies. But assuming that an embryo is already a human being (why, if this is the case, is it never buried religiously?) gives colossal power to men of the Church over women and, through them, over the whole of society.

THE CATHOLIC CHURCH'S OPPOSITION TO WOMEN'S EMANCIPATION

In the name of defending the "family" on all levels, sexual and social, the Roman magisterium returned to the developments of the Second Vatican Council. The latter, while developing a positive theology of conjugality and the sacrament of marriage, had refrained from legislating on the use of the contraceptive pill. In fact, the debate was not unanimous within the commissions, and this led Pope Paul VI (1963–1978), who was urged by some advisers, including Karol Wojtyla, the future John Paul II, to reserve the decision on the subject. Thus, in the conciliar constitution *Gaudium et Spes* 51, note 4 specifies that:

> By order of the Supreme Pontiff, certain questions which require further and more in-depth research have been entrusted to a Commission for the Problems of Population, the Family and Birth Rates, so that, once its role has been completed, the Pope may pronounce himself. Since the teaching of the Magisterium thus remains what it is, the Council does not intend to propose concrete solutions immediately.

When the sequel was known, it was a disappointment followed by an immense shock within the Catholic community. The commission would follow the future John Paul II and express firm opposition to a liberalization of contraception. But the encyclical *Humanae Vitae*, published on July 25, 1968, intended above all to reaffirm the competence of the magisterium, which alone was capable of interpreting the natural law and explaining the nature of marriage. The ecclesiastical hierarchy did not intend to dissociate sexual relations and procreation. To this end, the text specifies that "each and every marital act must of necessity retain its intrinsic relationship to the procreation of human life" (HV 11).

This encyclical had the effect of a bomb, not only on the experts who had not been followed, but on all Catholic opinion. In the parishes, it was rightly perceived as a slap in the face by Catholics who did not feel considered as adults in the faith. Women, who are concretely the first to have to face the weight of repeated births, understood that they were not heard. They gradually left the Church, and later, their children, whom they did not encourage toward adherence to a practice so disconnected from the truth of their lives, have done the same.

This pro-maternal voluntarism that characterized the pontificate of John Paul II came into direct conflict with the faith of many women. They did not see how their so-called proximity to the mother of Jesus, whose magisterium affirms that she is the mother of an only child, would have enjoined them to raise families that were too large to guarantee the well-being of their children. In this fight by the pope against the emancipation of women, Mary was not used wisely. In order to reject contemporary societal and medical advances, the pope drew an omnipresent and docile feminine image of Mary to definitively represent women. But we will soon see how far he has moved away from the portrait and expectations of the evangelists.

From his own hypotheses, John Paul II gradually built a doctrinal edifice around Mary. A domestic figure devoted to care and motherhood, she would play this role to the point of having to take on unacceptable excesses. Thus, for example, we have heard quite often over the last twenty years this masculine affirmation that was already present throughout history but that seemed to have disappeared with Vatican II: "We have Christ, you have Mary." This is more than an excusable shift; it is a theological misinterpretation. In addition to repeating the errors already mentioned about Mary as a model for women only, this division suggests that Mary would offer salvation to women, that she would therefore be God, and that Christ would be only a man and not the "new Adam," that is to say, the new humanity, man and woman. Would he then save only men? By dividing humanity into two halves, this expression gives men and women different destinies of salvation, which, of course, has no scriptural support. This is how an already deviant puppet clerical corpus is further swollen.

One can hope that Pope Francis's relative silence on the sexist construction of his predecessors was only motivated by the concern not to contradict them because neither the tone nor the substance of his thought was the same. If the tone was deliberately joking, it was not always well appreciated by women. Thus, this witticism, which dates from 2015: "Women are like strawberries on the cake: we always need more of them."[20] It is not surprising that Rita Amabili, a Quebec theologian, laments: "The strawberry that I am will always wonder if the Catholic Church will know in the near future that a woman is not a thing, but a human-equal."[21] In substance, however, Francis's thought deviates from that of his predecessors. He dwells less on the body of Mary, and therefore on the assignments made to women, than on the evangelizing function of Mary in the Church and in society:

> This dynamic of justice and tenderness, of contemplation and of walking toward others, is what makes [Mary] an ecclesial model for evangelization. We implore her that, through her maternal prayer, she may help us so that the Church may become a home for many. (EG 288)

Mary is for him this effective figure of the Church who, maternally, welcomes without discrimination. "Mary will always be a mixed-race Mother, because in her heart all people find a place, because love seeks all means to love and be loved."[22] In the same speech, however, he does not avoid gender comparisons:

> What would Peru be without mothers and grandmothers, what would our life be without them! Love for Mary must help us to have attitudes of recognition and gratitude toward women, toward our mothers and grandmothers who are a bulwark in the life of our cities.

Driven by this momentum, the pope even recognizes that "a woman, Mary, is more important than the bishops." According to him, this observation could "help to better recognize what this implies in relation to the possible role of women where important decisions are made, in the various environments of the Church" (EG 104).

In fact, Francis was able to take late and still cautious decisions in favor of women's access to governance of their Church. In April 2023, he granted, for the synod of October 2023, the right to vote to around fifty women, or a little more than 10 percent of the synodal assembly. This initiative shows that the discriminatory tendency is in decline in Rome. Women are no longer assigned a particular and unique vocation of wife and mother. The public sphere within the Church is no longer closed to them "on principle," even if the possibility of women's responsibility in sacramental matters is still a taboo subject.

At the end of this first part of our deconstruction, let us recall the surprising discovery that we have highlighted: Eve is not at all the cursed woman who brought about the "fall" of the couple and therefore of all humanity, but she is a rich and complex figure, full of nuances, a positive figure because of her intelligence and the creative capacity that she holds, but potentially exposed to excess. At the level of the ecclesiastical institution, we have also observed the incredible masculine determination, particularly under the pontificate of John Paul II, to keep women in the gilded cage of biological assignment. In defiance of the scriptures that the magisterium is nevertheless responsible for defending, the Church has reinforced an ideal image of "woman" that does not exist and that prevents us from seeing "real women," all different, who, like "real men," resist the assignments of convenience. Despite some overtures from Pope Francis, the road to equality is still long.

2

NUMQUAM SATIS[1]

DE MARIAE, NUMQUAM SATIS. Nothing will ever be too much for Mary, nothing is too beautiful, one must never stop praying to her....Saint Bernard's formula encompasses a number of situations, but it especially expresses the desire for "always more" about her. The history of the Marian cult in the West confirms this. Mary occupies a very large place there to which her many "gender" qualities predestined her. She is discreet, without a domineering will, able to hear all the pain, to sympathize, and in return, to deliver a message of hope. The popular piety that she has aroused over the centuries has therefore been considerable. We can even dare to say that the more violent societies have been, the more the figure of Mary has helped to neutralize and appease the surge of ambient brutality. And if piety toward Mary has been limitless, dogmatic discourse has been no less abundant. Before understanding the why and how of the dogmas that concern her, let us go to the very prolific cult of which she was the object, sometimes to the point of idolatry.

AN OVERFLOWING MARIAN PIETY

The Council of Ephesus, which opened in 431, is at the foundation of the inflations of Marian piety. It attributed to Mary the title "Mother of God." Before analyzing it, let us observe all the meanings, gestures, and places dedicated to Mary that this qualification offers. In its aftermath many Marian buildings were erected, the best-known example of which is Santa Maria Maggiore in Rome. Little by little, Marian feasts multiplied: her nativity, which originated in Jerusalem in the fourth century and was established in the West in the seventh century; the presentation of Mary in the temple, also initiated in Jerusalem, became especially important in the East. The feast of the assumption of Mary dates from the sixth century in the East, where it is called the "Dormition." It was later adopted in the West. As this veneration progressed, the vocabulary swelled with infinite compliments that revered Mary, who became both "the" Virgin and Queen of Heaven. The East is supremely fond of this piety. A Byzantine commentator is enthusiastic: "She is truly heaven, and even more than heaven, she is the one who contains the one whom no one can contain, and embraces the infinite."[2]

In Europe, the Middle Ages developed an extreme devotion to Mary. Cathedrals were often dedicated to her, and her festivals became so numerous that in the sixteenth century, Luther rebelled against these excesses. Later, the apparitions of the Virgin multiplied, generating many places of pilgrimage, notably in France, such as Lourdes, La Salette, and L'Île-Bouchard. In 2019, there were 2,900 places of pilgrimage to Mary active at least once a year. Although some of them are very modest, they nevertheless attest to Mary's great popularity. This devotion seems to have reached its peak in two events: the adoption of the dogma of the assumption in 1950 and the centenary of the adoption of the dogma of the immaculate conception in 1954.

Such devotion has certainly encouraged Marian dogmas. The veneration of the "three whites"—the pope, the host, and Mary—from a dream of Don Bosco in 1862 underlines the notion that, according to the Dominican Dominique Cerbelaud, "Mary personifies in some way the holiness of the entire Church,"[3] to the point where Yves Congar asks "if the Marian figure does not purely and simply incarnate the Roman Church."[4]

But this image of the Church's purity is strongly undermined by the revelation of abuses toward minors and people in vulnerable situations. The recent publication of the report of l'Arche[5] on the behavior of its founder Jean Vanier and Thomas Philippe, the Dominican who accompanied the movement, not only shatters the parallel with Mary but shows the extent of the delirium to which Marian devotion can lead, namely, that Philippe saw her, in an incestuous mysticism, uniting with her son.

On the side of the faithful, a strong relationship, also marked by the "never enough" mentioned here, has been established. That medals appear on necks and wrists, that statuettes are installed in houses or on front doors, that the name of Mary is generously given to children, nothing is more legitimate. The other monotheistic faiths also acknowledge their faith on their bodies or in familiar places. Mary offers a model of evangelical life that justifies the desire to place one's life under her protective wing.

The problem arises when the connection with scripture becomes strained or even disappears. Tradition has accumulated devotions that have become "obvious" even though they have no support in the Gospels. For example, the pietà, the scene in which Mary holds her dead son on her knees, goes back to the Middle Ages but has no scriptural support. Where in scripture do we see Mary weeping? Where do we see her as the confidant of souls tortured by sin? More questionable, where do we see her having the power to forgive, which is said to belong only to God (see Luke 5:21)?

Certainly, the reader's freedom must be respected. The reader has the right to fill in the blanks in the text, especially since they are quite often desired by the writer, either because the additional information is useless, or because they invite the reader to give them content. In the case of Mary, we will discover that the absence of information sometimes responded to a specific intention. But popular additions must not contradict scripture. How can we justify, in the light of scripture, the dissemination of miraculous medals and other famous ones? The direction is worrying when superstition gets involved. By dint of having the reputation of protecting those who pray to her, Mary becomes a talisman. She must save them from illness, accident, or catastrophe. That it is a support, a help, a comfort in times of trial is understandable, on condition that one does not fall into magic or superstition.

Above all, Mary must not take the place of Christ. However, most of these devotions generate a tenacious conviction, that of her quasi-divine omnipotence. This anecdote, already a century old, will illustrate it. It is the story of a postwoman from Briançon who discovers, during her rounds, that fire has broken out in her village. "Rushing toward the church, with a mail bag on her back, she takes the Virgin down from her altar and walks the streets shouting like a madwoman: 'Look! Look what you let happen!'"[6] Let us observe mischievously that this woman does not give up believing in Mary's divine character, but she implies that she did her job badly. Apart from the fact that today we would attribute these catastrophes more to human negligence than to divine will, we can see here that Mary took the place of Christ.

Another example of Marian adoration appears in the devotion to the Spanish Virgin of La Macarena. This seventeenth-century sculpture sits enthroned in a basilica in Seville dedicated to her. It is taken out during the Holy Week processions to be venerated in the streets of the city. Adorned like a queen with an immense golden crown, her bust adorned with impressive emeralds offered by the matadors of whom she is the godmother, she no longer has much in common with the young woman from Israel who welcomed Jesus. With a face bearing a smile mixed with tears, she presents herself as "compassionate and gentle, silent and adored," as Laure Charpentier writes in the presentation of her work *La Macarena. La Vierge qui pleure et qui console* (*The Macarena: The Virgin Who Weeps and Consoles*).[7] This exuberance in her presentation would quickly make one forget that she is certainly the mother of the Lord, but only his mother, not a goddess to be venerated for herself.

Even today in France, in certain baptismal celebrations, the multiplication of prayers to Mary and the laying of flowers that concludes the ceremony end up making us forget the meaning of this sacrament, the most fundamental for every Christian. Such veneration would have had no meaning in the first communities. However, for centuries and, increasingly, from the sixteenth to the twentieth centuries, it is the image of Mary, virgin, chaste, and pure, having been conceived without sin, that is privileged.

MARY AT THE SERVICE OF ECCLESIAL POLITICS

Let us recall that this primacy given to Mary over Christ has been condemned many times by the Church. More often than one might think, popular piety has surpassed the institution. This had to be affirmed again during the Second Vatican Council. Coming just ten years after the Marian apogee of the 1950s, this firm clarification shows the urgency and the extent of the abuses needing to be straightened out. The Council recalled that the Church preaches a single mediator, Christ: "For there is one God; there is also one mediator between God and humankind, Christ Jesus, himself human" (1 Tim 2:5). It also specifies:

> The Blessed Virgin is invoked in the Church under the titles of Advocate, Auxiliatrix, Adjutrix, and Mediatrix. This, however, is to be so understood that it neither takes away from nor adds anything to the dignity and efficaciousness of Christ the one Mediator. For no creature could ever be counted as equal with the Incarnate Word and Redeemer. (LG 62)

Let us also not forget that there is no treatise on Mary before the sixteenth century and that, until the nineteenth century, there are very few. The word *Mariology* does not appear until the seventeenth century. Furthermore, this term *Mariology* suggests that it would be distinct from *Christology*, as if to complete it, whereas it should be integrated with it.

How can we explain this recurring tropism toward exaggerated Marian piety once and for all? As we have already suggested, it is the triple consequence of: (1) a male domination that strives to magnify a figure previously placed in a position of submission; (2) the aspiration of certain clerics to find in this model of absolute purity *the* woman, whose dominant model is and will remain for them their mother; and (3) the need to offer a refuge to those who are in search of compassion. It is to all of them that the inflated image of the "Virgin Mary" provides support. How, then, can we be surprised by the excesses? And yet Mary would be so much closer, but also more sublime and more consoling, if she were stripped of these disguises and restored to her true role!

There may be another explanation, much more difficult to unearth but undoubtedly powerful. We have said that Mary is a political figure. This statement finds a new, worrying application today. Indeed, the figure of Mary who speaks little, who asks little, who bows before the will of God expressed by the clergy, fits very well with the traditionalist current, partly inspired by the polemicist Charles Maurras, that has been on the rise for several decades in the French Catholic Church. According to Maurras, who was condemned by Rome in 1914 for several of his works and in 1926 for his newspaper *L'Action française,* the gospel is dangerously subversive because it advocates the importance of the weak, which is contrary to the usual criteria of merit in society, and threatens the powerful. The text most hated by this author was the Magnificat, whose "venom" he castigated. Rather than Christ, the major reference of this current is the Church, charged above all with ensuring respect for the moral order. This observation is easy to verify in the speeches of the traditionalist movement. Christ is rarely mentioned there in favor of a discourse in which the words *God* and *Church* dominate.

A single example will illustrate the recent return of an omnipotent, almost deified Marian figure. It is the song *Regarde l'étoile* ("Look at the Stars").[8] The believer to whom it is addressed is overwhelmed by temptations, ambition, various passions, and very serious faults, and Mary is the star that rises over the sea and lights up the whole world. "She will lead you to the port," concludes the refrain without any reference to Christ. This omission confirms the desire to propose a Marian figure much less radical than Christ, because she will have previously been assigned the gender codes that want her to be submissive, humble, and, above all, silent. If she shows herself to be particularly compassionate toward sinners, while the Gospel never alludes to a particular predilection of Mary toward them, could it not be because blame and guilt are at the center of the hold on the faithful desired by these currents of thought?

Also, in the traditionalist "star system," Mary, as long as she forgets the Magnificat, is by far preferable to her son. And the more she eclipses him, the better. The clergy will then only have to have the good news carried by Mary, a figure entirely remodeled according to their expectations.

ON THE GOOD AND BAD USE OF DOGMAS

It was under the effect of the sixteenth-century Catholic Reformation that a quasi-divinization of Mary was established, the theological path of which we will describe. Louis-Marie Grignion de Montfort (1673–1716) introduced a word that would flourish, that of "mediatrix."[9] Mary, he maintained, is like a mediatrix with Christ the mediator. Alphonsus Liguori (1696–1787), a Doctor of the Church and founder of the Redemptorists, explained that all graces come to us through the hands of Mary, and he already held as certain the doctrine of the Immaculate Conception, which he wished to see defined as a dogma of faith, which happened in 1854.[10]

But inflation does not stop. In the twentieth century, the Polish Franciscan Maximilian Kolbe (murdered at Auschwitz and canonized in 1982) reached new heights. He founded a spiritual movement called "The Mission of the Immaculate" and dedicated his life to Mary. We read from his pen: "It can be affirmed that the Immaculate is, in a certain sense, the incarnation of the Holy Spirit."[11]

This passion for Mary has also been shared by the liberation theologian Leonardo Boff (born 1938), who rooted his commitment to the poor of Latin America in his veneration of Mary. He writes in particular: "The Virgin Mary...must be considered as hypostatically united to the third Person of the Holy Trinity." And he continues: "Just as the Word, hypostatically united to the man Jesus, divinizes the masculine, so the Holy Spirit divinizes the feminine in Mary."[12]

The term *hypostatic* used by Boff deserves an explanation, because it has caused much ink to flow since the first centuries of Christianity. *Hypóstasis* in Greek (like its Latin translation *substantia*) expresses "that which is held at the foundation," either of a principle or of a person. Concerning the Trinity—Father, Son, and Spirit—the great councils, by using this term, wanted to signify the way in which these three persons interact in a type of union that respects both their own identity and their relationships.

By integrating Mary into these trinitarian relationships, Boff adds an additional complication. On the one hand, as Dominique Cerbelaud points out: "It is not to the masculine that the Word is united hypostatically but to human nature!"[13] So, there is no point in adding the already present feminine. On the other hand, these admirers of Mary among the liberation theologians took the great risk of creating a "quaternity" in place of the Trinity. By maintaining that Mary is united hypostatically to the Spirit, Leonardo Boff makes her the equal of the Spirit and the Word; she shares with them the same foundation; she is of the same family. But this development deifies Mary, which is a heresy.

MARY COREDEMPTRIX?

In the wake of this trend toward exaggeration, pressure was exerted around 1950 on Pius XII, who had just promulgated the dogma of the assumption. Some even came to wish that Mary be declared "coredemptrix." We see that the adage already mentioned—*De Mariae, numquam satis*— dies hard. It is as if faith in one God was decidedly unable to penetrate the hearts of human beings!

This idea of coredemption is not new; it was born in the sixteenth century, doubtless blown by the wind of the Catholic Reformation, which wanted to restore to Mary a prestige that the Protestants contested. Five centuries later, Maximilian Kolbe took it up again. But theologians are very divided on this point and, as we have already said, the Second Vatican Council, after much discussion, decided not to treat Mariology in itself but instead devoted only chapter 8 of its Constitution on the Church to it.

The Council fathers considered simply that Mary's situation did not call for any new dogma. This decision raises the question of the precise definition of a dogma. A dogma is a statement in which the Church recognizes a valid expression of its faith.

Once adopted, it is authoritative. The first "ecumenical" councils, those composed of bishops from "all the inhabited earth,"[14] established the principal foundations of the profession of faith in matters where scripture did not provide a clear answer.

These first councils had as their object to define who Christ was. These councils are the Council of Nicaea in 325, which declared Jesus to be consubstantial (of the same nature) with the Father, the Council of Constantinople (381), which dealt with the Holy Spirit and the Trinity, the Council of Ephesus (431), and that of Chalcedon in 451, which recognized Christ, true God and true man in one person.

Four Dogmas of Mary

The Catholic Church has four dogmas regarding Mary that, according to the magisterium, every Catholic is required to believe. The last was promulgated in 1950.

The first is based on the Council of Ephesus, which met in 431. It declared Mary the Mother of God (*Theotokos*).

Later, in 649, the Lateran Synod under Pope Martin I formulated the dogma of the perpetual virginity of Mary, which decreed that Mary had no sexual relations with her husband Joseph during their entire married life.

Much later, in 1854, Pius IX, on his own initiative, promulgated the bull *Ineffabilis Deus*, which decreed the immaculate conception to be a dogma. Adopted in 1870 by the bishops of the First Vatican Council, this dogma teaches that "the most Blessed Virgin Mary, in the first instant of her conception, by a singular grace and privilege granted by Almighty God, in view of the merits of Jesus Christ, the Savior of the human race, was preserved free from all stain of original sin" and that this is a revelation from God.[15] This insistence on the conception of Mary (and no longer of Jesus!) intends to show that Mary's life is the summit of holiness.

Finally, in 1950, Pius XII promulgated the dogma of the assumption, which "affirms, declares and defines as a divinely revealed dogma, that the Immaculate Mother of God, the ever Virgin Mary, having completed the course of her earthly life, was assumed body and soul into heavenly glory."[16]

In addition to the four dogmas devoted to Mary, the Second Vatican Council had considered the possibility of a "fifth Marian dogma," that of "Mary coredemptrix." And in fact, a party of Catholics remained attached to this devotion and theology prior to Vatican II. But the Council recalled that Christ is the only redeemer, and that Mary could not be coredemptrix. It referred the debate to a commission that was finally formed in 1996. Fifteen theologians met in Czestochowa, Poland, and, despite a very academic and very measured vocabulary, unanimously decided:

> As proposed, the titles appear ambiguous, because they can be understood in different ways. It has also become apparent that one must not abandon the theological line followed by the Second Vatican Council, which did not wish to define any of them. In its magisterium, it did not use the word *co-redemptrix* and it made very sparing use of the titles of *mediatrix* and *advocate.* In reality, the term *co-redemptrix* has not been used by the magisterium of the sovereign pontiffs, in important documents, since the time of Pius XII....Finally, theologians, especially non-Catholic theologians, have shown themselves sensitive to the ecumenical difficulties that a definition of these titles would entail.[17]

The pontifical academy in charge of Marian questions therefore took note that there was no need for a new dogma. And Cardinal Joseph Ratzinger, then prefect of the Congregation for the Doctrine of the Faith, confirmed that this "concept of *co-redemptrix* deviates from both scripture and patristic writings."[18] Therefore no fifth Marian dogma was declared.

For the record, no verse of the four Gospels can provide the slightest basis for the Immaculate Conception or the Assumption. In this case, the Church has defined these specific doctrines on foundations other than scripture. Such anchoring of these dogmas is acceptable only on the condition that it does not contradict the Gospel, which would obviously be the case with the title of "mediatrix," which is incompatible with the Epistle to Timothy that makes Christ the only mediator (see 1 Tim 2:5).

Furthermore, since the end of the first millennium, the "dogmatic" councils[19] have become more questionable because they have been less and less "ecumenical." Bishops have been absent from the roll call, particularly in 1870 at Vatican I, because of the war that disrupted its course. But above all, since the schism of 1054 between the Latin West and the Greek East of Byzantium, the bishops of the East have no longer attended. And as we have already emphasized, it was by his authority alone that Pope Pius IX by the bull *Ineffabilis Deus* established the celebration of the Immaculate Conception in 1854 and instituted it as dogma in 1870, using his brand-new papal infallibility. These four dogmas forge the veneration of Mary by the faithful.

A JUSTIFICATION: "DOGMATIC EXTENSION"

The work of a male magisterium, this sacralization of Mary, the ever-virgin mother who has never sinned, arouses some suspicion. For such feminists as Uta Ranke-Heineman,[20] it may be the fruit of the maternal idealization experienced by celibate clerics. The fact that Mary is at the same time the mother of Jesus and, when she symbolizes the Church, the wife of Christ does not seem to trouble them. What a platform!

Thus, relying on an aspiration that is more psychological than theological, the clergy make Mary play all the roles. As they make Mary the model for all women, they expose them to a totally unrealistic representation of themselves.

Does this mean that we should reject the dogmas concerning Mary? An international theological commission that met in 1989 explained: "The Second Vatican Council has...highlighted the historical dimension of dogmas. It teaches that the people of God in their entirety participate in the prophetic office of Christ and that, with the help of the Holy Spirit, there is in the Church a progress in the understanding of the apostolic tradition," that is, of what the evangelists and the first Christian generations have transmitted to us.

These lines justify what the Church calls "dogmatic extension," according to which it is possible to affirm over the centuries truths of faith that were not present in the Gospels. Furthermore, this commission confirms that the denial of the dogmas of the Church "is rejected as heresy and punished by anathema."[21] Such an affirmation is worrying because, on the one hand, the faithful were not consulted;[22] on the other hand, it imprisons them in rigid formulations. It is also useful to refer to what great theologians say about it, such as Bernard Sesboüé or Walter Kasper. The latter explains, for his part, that a dogma of the Church is never a proposition that would totally encompass and exhaust the object in question. According to him, a dogma is "not only the conclusion of a discussion, but always also a new beginning."[23] Finally, Pope Francis recalls that "true religion is not a freezer, and doctrine is not static; it grows and develops like a tree."[24]

It is therefore permissible to question tradition and dogmas in a Church called to constant growth, since it is founded on a "living" tradition that can authorize the questioning of certain aspects of dogmas while never losing sight of the view that only Christ saves, as Peter reminds the Jewish leaders after the healing of a cripple:

> Let it be known to all of you, and to all the people of Israel, that this man is standing before you in good health by the name of Jesus Christ of Nazareth, whom you crucified, whom God raised from the dead. This Jesus is "the stone that was rejected by you, the builders; it has become the cornerstone." There is salvation in no one else, for there is no other name under heaven given among mortals by which we must be saved. (Acts 4:10–12)

Two Examples of Dogmatic Extension

The two Marian dogmas of the immaculate conception and the assumption illustrate the notion of "dogmatic extension." Nothing proclaims them in scripture. If we seek to give them an acceptable content today, we must first of all dismiss the false idea that the conception of Mary who, being "immaculate," would be removed from the sexual relations proper to all human beings. As the text specifies that "the most Blessed Virgin Mary, in the first instant of her conception, was...preserved from all stain of original sin," it is then possible to consider only the question of original sin. Without entering into such a vast and controversial subject, the conclusion of this dogmatic exposition would be to show that the life of Mary is the summit of holiness.

The dogma of the assumption, for its part, places images on the last judgment granted to Mary: to join "body and soul in the heavenly glory." In both cases, these dogmas testify to the recognition by the Church of the exemplary life of Mary, the one who believed and was faithful to Christ. But in both cases, these dogmas seek to exonerate Mary from all "impurity," in particular that of the passage through death from which Christ himself was not exempted. While the Western Church holds that Mary actually died before being assumed into heaven, the Eastern Church uses the term "dormition" to indicate the belief that Mary did not die but only "fell asleep." This theme of purity runs through all Marian ideology; we will explore it further.

In conclusion, let us recall that Mary, the very one who gave human flesh to the Word, the one who, at Cana, urged Jesus to perform his first sign, thereby revealing him as *sent*, this Mary has no need to be artificially divinized to find her place and guide anyone in the faith. Therefore, against an unreasonable and unfounded divinization that locks Mary into a veneration close to heresy, it is important to remain faithful to what she did in an exemplary manner in the Gospels.

But before arriving at this part of our investigation, let us ask ourselves what is expressed by this title so often given to Mary, that of "Holy Virgin."

3

VIRGINITY IN QUESTION

AMONG THE FOUR Marian dogmas that we have just cited, one of them concerns the virginity of Mary. This is the dogma of her perpetual virginity,[1] promulgated in 649, according to which she and Joseph abstained from sexual relations during their entire married life.

This statement sounds very much like a male fantasy. On the one hand, it proves a great ignorance of the First Testament that the magisterium has the mission to teach, and on the other hand, it reveals a confused understanding that must be clarified. Let us try to give substance to our somewhat harsh criticism by closely analyzing the biblical texts, the contributions of the prophets, and the ecclesiastical commentaries. Then let us consider all the negative consequences that women have had to suffer because of this absolute understanding of virginity.

WHAT THE GOSPELS SAY

Only two evangelists, Matthew and Luke, address the question of Mary's virginity, and they approach it very differently. Matthew surprises his reader in his first chapter by concluding the genealogy of Jesus with this sentence: "Jacob the father of Joseph the husband of Mary, of whom Jesus was born" (Matt

1:16). By omitting to say that Joseph is the father, he prepares for the announcement of the virginal conception of Jesus.

Matthew starts from Joseph's experience: "Before they lived together, she was found to be with child from the Holy Spirit" (Matt 1:18). Faced with the unacceptable prospect of a relationship outside of marriage, Joseph plans to divorce his fiancée. But a dream dissuades him: "Do not be afraid to take Mary as your wife, for the child conceived in her is from the Holy Spirit" (1:20). What will Joseph do? Accede, with courage, as Matthew suggests to him. Instead of repudiating his fiancée, he agrees, on the contrary, to "[take] her as his wife" (1:24), because it is revealed to him that "the child conceived" comes from the Spirit.

Like other biblical personages, Joseph is a "character," that is to say, he represents more than his own existence. Matthew, in fact, gives him a special function. He describes him as a "just man." Implicitly, the evangelist takes sides. For him, Joseph belongs to the great family of the just ones of Israel who consented to the manifestation of God. The deduction was not so obvious, however, since, as the *TOB* reports,[2] Saint Jerome himself wondered how Joseph could be described as just when he "hides his wife's crime." More just than Jerome would be, Matthew has decided between the legalistic interpretation and the spiritual understanding and seems to say to his reader: "You, too, be just, with that justice that discerns good beyond the established rule." This short story highlights Matthew's great talent as a storyteller, put here to the service of a major endeavor: to show how, through Joseph's conversion, God sends a savior who comes through unusual means, that of the Spirit.

Matthew then appeals to an oracle of the prophet Isaiah to inform Joseph and support his story: "Look, the young woman is with child and shall bear a son, and shall name him Immanuel" (Isa 7:14). The Greek word *parthenos*, which appears in the quotation, supports Matthew's point. It is all the more interesting because it has evolved over the course of translations. In the Hebrew Bible, the expression used by Isaiah is "young woman." As a note in the *TOB* explains about this translation, the term *parthenos* in Matthew was interpreted by Christian tradition as "meaning 'virgin' and applied to Mary, the mother of Jesus. But the ancient Greek version also rendered by the same word *parthenos*, the Hebrew terms designating a young woman (Gen 24:43; Isa 7:14) or a young girl (Gen 24:14–16)." Both the NRSVCE and the *TOB* translate it as "the young woman."[3]

The tradition of the Church saw in this a meaning worthy of being preserved in that it goes without saying that a young girl is a virgin. The title of "virgin," therefore, enters into the story. Matthew's remarks end with an important piece of information for our subject: Joseph "had no marital relations with her until she had borne a son" (1:25). Joseph agrees to abstain from sexual relations. Even in his body, he inscribes a withdrawal intended for the work of the Spirit to be accomplished.

This story therefore teaches that the Spirit raises up a savior in the body of Mary, with the active consent of Joseph. The attestation of the young woman's virginity is at the service of this project of salvation. And the verse gives a limit to abstinence: "until she had borne a son."

Luke, for his part, reports in the story of the annunciation (see Luke 1:26–38) that an "engaged virgin" is informed, not by a dream, but by an angel, that she "will conceive." This association says a lot. The betrothal announces the wedding while virginity shows the condition. Indeed, for Israel, female virginity is indispensable if a marriage is to be permitted. To speak of an "engaged virgin" is superfluous. All young girls get engaged in a state of virginity. This becomes the antechamber to marriage since it is not there for herself, but "in view" of the wedding. Moreover, Luke's account clearly shows that Mary does not manifest any aspiration to virginity for herself. She asks: "How can this be, since I am a virgin?" (1:34). The angel answers her: "The Holy Spirit will come upon you, and the power of the Most High will overshadow you" (1:35). Like Matthew, Luke shows the conversion to which the young woman is called, but he insists more on the "yes" that she will pronounce and on the greatness of God, recalling the prophetic word: "Is anything too hard for me?" (Jer 32:27).

If Matthew and Luke attest that the conception of Jesus took place when Mary was a virgin and that this conception did not change her virginity, they infer further: It took more than a man's seed to ensure the coming of this child. It took the Spirit. This information also allows Mary and Joseph to become aware of their exceptional parental vocation, which is to educate the Savior. But let us observe carefully that neither in the infancy Gospels nor elsewhere in the New Testament is there any question of a virginity that extends beyond the birth of the child.

Brothers and Sisters of Jesus

The dogma of Mary's perpetual virginity excludes the existence of brothers and sisters. However, if the Jewish logic of the time is to see virginity as a necessary and transitory state, we can welcome without contention the Gospel information about Jesus's brothers and sisters. There are indeed numerous references to Jesus's siblings: "His mother and his brothers" (Mark 3:31; Matt 2:46–50; Luke 8:19–21); "Is not his mother called Mary? And are not his brothers James and Joseph and Simon and Judas? And are not all his sisters with us?" (Matt 13:55–56); "his brothers" (John 7:3); "with his brothers" (Acts 1:14); "the brothers of the Lord" (1 Cor 9:5); "James, the Lord's brother" (Gal 1:19). There are no fewer than nine occurrences.

The Greek word *adelphos*, "brother," used here, can also evoke a "cousin" or a close relative. However, Greek already has a term for "cousin," *anepsios*, as well as two other terms for half-brother on the mother's or father's side. There is therefore no reason to exclude a flesh-and-blood fraternity from the vocabulary used. Furthermore, if the evangelists had wanted to signify permanent virginity, they would not have taken the risk of this confusion by mentioning brothers and sisters of Jesus. For them, the subject does not raise any controversy.

In reality, nothing in the New Testament insists on the theme of Mary's virginity beyond the birth of Jesus—he "had no marital relations with her until she had borne a son" (Matt 1:25). Later, the maintenance of this state would be anthropologically incomprehensible in the surrounding universe since the place of every woman in the household consisted first of all in giving sons to her husband.

Orthodox tradition considers that Joseph had sons and daughters from a first marriage. But we can then wonder why, in the quotes just mentioned, these brothers and sisters are associated with Mary and not with Joseph, and why the text does not use the appropriate words since they exist. Catholicism, for its part, chooses to think that the word *adelphos* here designates cousins, little differentiated from biological brothers and sisters in the Semitic usage of the time. Finally, for Protestants, Mary and Joseph had other children after the birth of Jesus. However, Calvin, for his part, recommended not to make this act of faith, which deserves respect, "a subject of curiosity contrary to Scripture." We can agree with him in considering that it is not appropriate to restrict what has above all a theological value to an event with magical connotations.

VIRGINITY IN THE ANCIENT WORLD

To understand what fueled the words of Luke and Matthew, we must know the mores of their culture as dependent on both their environment and the First Testament. Let us first recall that, for ancient Israel, virginity is a complex notion, affected by several meanings. First, as we have already mentioned, it is both necessary and transitory. Under penalty of death, young marriageable girls must preserve their virginity until their marriage. But remaining a virgin is a curse since it is incompatible with motherhood, which is the feminine vocation in all ancient cultures.

The most eloquent biblical example is that of Jephthah's daughter. Jephthah, to thank God for having allowed him to win a war, vowed to offer as a burnt offering the first person who greeted him when he returned home. This was his only child, his daughter. Learning of her fate, the young girl asked to retire to the mountain to "bewail [her] virginity" (Judg 11:37). She thus expresses her misfortune at dying a virgin, which would have deprived her of motherhood.

Another, more positive view, however, appears around the first century, particularly at Qumran. Virginity, both masculine and feminine, attests to purity. It becomes an element of the ascetic spiritualities that developed at the time and that would soon become popular with the Stoic philosophical movements and the currents opposed to sexuality, marriage, and procreation, which are called "Encratism."[4]

Finally, in parallel with this trend that was gradually establishing itself, the desire of the ancients to surround the births of great men with a certain mystery can explain the recourse to virginity. One type of writing: The *Lives*, such as that of Alexander the Great, for example, have the hero born miraculously from a virgin. It is therefore not forbidden to think that the stories of Jesus's childhood can present, in the choice of their themes and the way in which they are constructed, aspects borrowed from the ancient *Lives*. Their authors wanted to explain the exception, to tell the story in a grandiose way and, perhaps also, to establish the power of the one whose journey they are recounting. But their aim is not to relate historically precise facts. The marvelous is almost, for them, a narrative modality. Not only do they not understand the history literally, but it is not the object of belief. We see the trace of this state of mind in a commentary by Justin, an "apologist" of the Church of the first centuries, who relativizes the virginity of Mary precisely because he understands it in his usual framework of thought. He says this about Christ: "It is said that he was born of a virgin, like Perseus." This is to recognize that he attributes this virgin birth to a myth, without thereby disqualifying it but, on the contrary, to valorize it.

For our modern mentalities, confronted with scientific rationality, maintaining a critical distance toward the marvels of the *Lives* requires an effort. It exists, however, among historians and even among the educated public. They understand very well that this type of discourse aims to magnify an extraordinary destiny, and not to keep a precise chronicle of the facts.

On the other hand, in the Christian world, a critical distance regarding the way in which the birth of Jesus is told seems difficult to maintain. It tends to fade away in favor of a more fundamentalist reading, which clings to the material meaning of virginity. Some commentators, relying on this literal interpretation, value its miraculous aspect, while a good part of common opinion would like, in the name of modernity and a certain rationality, to erase from the Christian corpus any reference to virginity.

It is also necessary to recall how the question of virginity is treated in the First Testament, especially among the prophets. There we observe a fairly frequent and somewhat enigmatic formula, that of the "virgin of Israel." The prophet Jeremiah evokes this virgin, either to blame her saying, "The virgin Israel has done a most horrible thing" (Jer 18:13), or to praise her: "I have loved you with an everlasting love [says the Lord],...and you shall be built, O virgin Israel" (Jer 31:3), before exhorting her to return to love: "Return, O virgin Israel, return to these your cities!" (Jer 31:21). Another prophet, Joel, intones the same theme (see Joel 1:8), and the Book of Lamentations worries: "To what can I liken you, that I may comfort you, O virgin daughter Zion?" (Lam 2:13).

Clearly, virginity is used in a metaphorical sense here. It is the quality that God asks of the people of Israel because God loves them and expects the same love in return. This love is expressed through a nuptial language that is based on the two realities of married life already mentioned: betrothal and virginity. God is the bridegroom; the people will be the bride. God is engaged to the people who must receive God in a "virginal manner."

In the context of the prophets' fierce struggles against idols, virginity consisted of preserving oneself from false gods and their false prophets who defile the people by asking them to worship trees and wooden statues, stupefying those who serve them. Virginity is therefore a spiritual injunction. It says: "Let us remain in the Lord!" We can already deduce that remaining a virgin concerns both the women and the men of Israel.

For each, it becomes a matter of the heart and not of biology. The goal is to remain faithful to the one God. If the people are unfaithful, they risk that God will choose another people. In short, their spiritual virginity conditions their security. We can measure the extreme symbolic importance of virginity in tension with a reality that denies it: With the infidelities of the people who follow another god, the virginity of Israel is constantly soiled. But, as every reader of the Bible knows, God never carries out his threat. God is faithful; the betrothal is always "reoffered." This is what is expressed by this promise of the Talmud: The virgin has fallen, but she "will not do it again,"[5] because she has before her a wedding, always to be consummated, the covenant proposed to the people.

In short, the image of the "virgin of Israel" enriches the great prophetic theme of nuptial spirituality that speaks of the loving bond that exists between God and his people. Virginity speaks of availability to God. However, if it happened that Israel remained a virgin for too long without marrying her God (that is, without choosing him as her husband and therefore without loving him), then Israel would be nothing more than an "old maid." Virginity, instead of being a compliment, would become a reproach. A Canadian exegete, Micheline Gagnon, considers it to be a "reproach from the Lord to an Israel that is failing to give birth to the expected Messiah."[6] The objective becomes clear: It will be a question of giving birth through faith and action.

Thus, the tradition of Israel sheds a bright light on the accounts of Luke and Matthew. To describe the coming of the Savior Jesus as a new wedding, they had at their disposal a perfect figure that signified Israel: the Virgin.

CHRISTIAN COMMENTATORS ON VIRGINITY

One might expect Christian commentators to offer a spiritual reading of Mary's virginity. How did they speak of it? The first Christian author to mention it is Ignatius of Antioch (100 CE): "The virginity of Mary, the birth of her child, and the death of the Lord are three resounding mysteries which were accomplished in the silence of God."[7] From this enthusiastic declaration, what can we deduce? Very little, at first glance, but of great significance. First of all, let us question these unusual equivalences. The virginity of Mary is here on the same level as the death of Jesus. If we remain within the categories of thought of ancient Israel—which is likely for Ignatius, who lived before the definitive rupture between Jews and Christians—this virginity must have as its object the expression of the love for God to which Israel can finally bear witness. It says that Israel, personified by Mary, loves its God. Ignatius is announcing truly good news. Within the same symbolism, childbirth, for its part, would imply the wedding; the fertility of this love and death would be the victory over evil.

Let us also remember that the meaning of the word *mystery* is not that of a marvel but rather is an invitation always to advance better and further toward the divine. As for silence, it expresses respect before the work of God. It perhaps also warns against a form of indecency in wanting to explain what must be received without chatter. In short, Ignatius thus summarizes the essence of the Christian message while remaining in the typology of the prophets, by inviting hearts to rejoice in love (virginity), marriage (childbirth), and salvation (the death of the Lord). If this spiritual interpretation of Ignatius is well-founded, it rules out a biological interpretation.

During the first centuries, the discussion on this theme gradually expanded, while the richness of prophetic virginity was lost. In the Christian galaxy, the idea of lasting virginity gradually took hold. To the initial virginity (*ante partum*) were added the notions of virginal childbirth (*virginitas in partu*) and perpetual virginity (*post partum*).

It was Clement of Alexandria in the third century who "invented" the concept of *virginitas in partu,* from apocryphal texts.[8] In the fourth century, a movement advocated for consecrated virgins (women!) and, with Athanasius of Alexandria, gave them Mary as a model. Within the same movement, Athanasius affirms that "virgins marry Christ."[9] We see how the prophetic theme, using a poetic and symbolic form applicable to all, is giving way to a sexual application of the nuptial metaphor that collapses its depth. Virginity is now only physical and feminine. Using and misusing the difference between generations, Ephrem dares to speak of "Mary, sister, wife and servant of Christ,"[10] and Gregory of Nazianzus invites women to cultivate virginity in order to become "mothers of Christ."[11] We see that men are beginning to worry about the materiality of the female body, a subject that is never addressed as such by the scriptures. As a result, confusion sets in; it is biological virginity—that of women—that will allow the spiritual birth of Christ.

Origen, however, persists in saying: "It is not only in Mary, it is in you that the Word of God must be born."[12] These divergent quotes expose a double discourse: Some of the early fathers continue to understand virginity in a spiritual way while others invest in and even prolong the image in a material way and make the figure of Mary a model for all women. Let us remember that it is a major flaw in reasoning to associate physical virginity with spiritual motherhood. The two attributes each apply within their order. The Church remembered this when it condemned Origen's sexual self-mutilation on the grounds that a spiritual provision should not be taken literally. Why did it forget it so quickly when it came to women?

When Gregory of Nyssa (fourth century) focuses on this question of virginity and makes the first mention of a "vow of virginity" of Mary, we understand that the "Jewish DNA" of this virginity is being lost. With him, and in the same period, the great thurifers of this movement will be Ambrose, Jerome, and especially Augustine, who defend Mary's perpetual virginity.

Amplifying these voices by a synod in 380, Pope Siricius excommunicated those who claimed that Mary and Joseph led the married life of everyone after the birth of Jesus. And since this pope also supports virginity during childbirth, the cause is heard. The ground on which a dogmatic decision will prosper is already plowed.

WHAT DOES MARY'S VIRGINITY MEAN?

Let us now take a step back to consider what meaning we can give to Mary's virginity. Her uniqueness, as we have already mentioned, is to be more than the virginity of a young girl before her wedding. Matthew says that Joseph "had no marital relations with her until she had borne a son" (Matt 1:25). What is at stake is therefore the "virginal conception of Jesus" and the absence of sexual relations during Mary's pregnancy. How can we understand them? We can offer two interpretations that are not mutually exclusive. The first fulfills the ancient tropism for stories of important births. It says that God can do anything, even raise up a child in the womb of a woman who has not known a man. This is, of course, a word of faith, not an article of science. The second is to connect with the prophetic current that sees in virginity the expectation of the wedding of all Israel with the Messiah. Mary's pregnancy will be that image. And the birth of the child, as Ignatius of Antioch suggested, is the consummation of the wedding: The Messiah is here! If this current insists on virginity, it is to magnify the marriage. In this case, virginity is the spiritual injunction that Mary obeyed. In both approaches, what is a dead end is to seek this virginity in Mary's body. The evangelists, faithful to the prophets, place themselves in a symbolic register with a theological aim. Virginity has nothing to say about Mary; it speaks of the Messiah, fruit of the wedding, whom we are invited to follow.

To understand this strictly religious issue, let us return to the story of the misadventure experienced by the midwife Salome related in the apocryphal gospel the *Protevangelium of James.*

The scene takes place as Joseph has gone to fetch a midwife for Mary, even though delivery has already taken place:

> And Salome said, As the Lord my God lives, unless I put my finger into it and examine its nature, I will never believe that a virgin has given birth. And the midwife came in and said, Mary, prepare yourself; for this is no small dispute that is being opened about you. And Mary, having heard this, prepared herself. And Salome put her finger into her nature. And Salome cried out and said, "Woe to my iniquity and my unbelief, because I have tempted the living God! And behold, my hand, consumed by fire, is detached from me." And Salome bowed her knees before the Master, saying, "God of my fathers, remember me, that I am of the seed of Abraham, Isaac, and Jacob. Do not make me an example to the children of Israel, but give me to the poor. For you know, Master, that in your name I worked my healings and that it was from you that I received my reward." And behold, an angel of the Lord appeared to her, saying, "Salome, Salome, the Master of all things has heard your prayer. Put your hand to the child and take him in your arms, and he will be to you salvation and joy. "And Salome, filled with joy, went to the child and took him in her arms, saying: "I will worship him, for he is the one who has been born king over Israel." And immediately

Salome was healed, and she went out justified from the cave.[13]

This very concrete text illustrates better than long speeches the impasse, the very deception, of the "gynecological track." Salome took the matter literally, like those fundamentalists who follow the letter and not the spirit. But she is punished for it in her body. The image clearly says how much mistakes of this type impoverish and even mutilate those who commit them. As soon as she turns to the child, Salome regains the use of her hand; she is absolved. The lesson of this little episode is clear: Let us turn away from an unhealthy curiosity about Mary in order to look at Jesus. It is Christ who heals. In fact, neither Luke nor Matthew praise virginity for its own sake. They use it as a narrative device (Matthew) or a literary genre (Luke) that allows them to magnify a future event and to celebrate the one who is at its center, Jesus.

The virginal conception of Jesus announces that God reveals Godself, that God comes to love, by sending the Son to a people who "keep themselves" for God alone. And, provided that we understand both the context and the purpose, it makes sense. We therefore affirm that there is more to lose by rejecting the concept of virginity than by using it. Yes, Mary is the virgin of Israel visited by a God whose love surpasses all that can be imagined.

Should we conclude that Mary and Joseph never shared a sexual life, as the Catholic Church teaches? In the Jewish context of the time, when marital relations were considered an honor to be rendered to God, the question may never have occurred to Luke and Matthew. On the other hand, against the historicist current of the 1970s, which deconstructed the virginal conception in the name of scientific rationality, it seems important to us to respect Matthew's affirmation quoted just now. It speaks of the power of God, while Mary's virginity during her pregnancy shows her spiritual availability "in view of the Son." If this virginity of Mary is a symbol, whether the couple had sexual relations or not becomes a useless curiosity.

A TRAGEDY THAT SPREADS AND NEVER ENDS

In the face of this story, we see how much commentators have neglected to take an interest in the cultural contexts of the evangelical writers. Curiously, the Catholic world, while it sometimes evokes "the daughter of Zion," not only does not draw any lessons from the expression "virgin of Israel" to express the love that exists between the people and their God but also does not use it to try to understand the virginity of Mary. For example, it is barely mentioned in a reference work such as Xavier Léon-Dufour's *Vocabulary of Biblical Theology*.

Would the Catholic Church not have avoided certain misunderstandings if it had understood virginity's evocative power? Why did it forget the prophets who speak of the love between God and God's people through the figure of a wedding whose bride must remain "virgin from idols" because this virginity guarantees her love? Why did it take so little account of the fact that, in Jewish tradition, virginity is a necessary but passing state? How did it not see that the central subject of the evangelists is to speak not of the magic of a supernatural birth but of the greatness of this divine child?

Perhaps these failings should be attributed to the violence of relations between the Jewish and Christian communities that could be observed from the second century until an almost complete rupture took place at the end of Antiquity. These dissensions distanced the young Christian Church from a healthy acquaintance with the First Testament. A few generations were enough for her to lose the ability to read "in the Jewish way" and, at the same time, to misunderstand its theological springs. The abyss that had opened up between the Christian communities and the Jewish communities compromised the transmission. It is a tragedy that has generated many dead ends or misinterpretations, of which the figure of Mary is undoubtedly the most telling example. Not only has Mary been misunderstood, but she is emblematic of other deviations concerning the interpretation of scripture.

Another factor, of a historical nature, may have also contributed to magnifying the physical virginity of women. In the Roman Empire, virginity may have been experienced as a positive state. It allowed many women to avoid the guardianship of a husband. The Church encouraged this form of emancipation. Also, in the minds of the Church fathers, encouraging virginity may not have been considered as an amputation of freedom for women but, on the contrary as a means of guaranteeing it.

In the following centuries, the Church, having become a temporal power, politicized the figure of Mary. Thus, to clerics whom the Gregorian Reform (eleventh century) established as pillars of the Church and on whom celibacy was imposed (twelfth century), the figure of an ever-virgin Mary was welcome. Perpetual virginity made it possible to preserve a clergy that unconsciously remained fixed on a pre-Oedipal maternal *imago*. It guarantees a priest that his mother will be his forever. Also, by exalting Mary, the ecclesiastical institution satisfies the body of priests on which it wanted to be based. But it ignores its vocation to be the Church of all, not only of the clergy, but of all the baptized, women and men. Here we see in all its magnitude the disaster caused by an institution that, to satisfy its "personnel," denies its primary quality, that of being the people of God. It is failing its own profound vocation.

In this political decision, the big losers were obviously women, and this has been the case since the end of Antiquity. We have seen that a fundamentalist reading gave them virginity as a model. Later, the institution offered lay women only the ascetic spirituality of nuns. We have forgotten that, according to the scriptures, Mary remains a metaphorical virgin because she keeps herself from idols. However, to envision virginity and motherhood in the literal sense as simultaneous and then permanent states is to go toward the madness of a double contradictory injunction. Also, for a woman who is aware of and listens to herself, it is preferable to flee simply to remain in good mental health.

All kinds of damage have resulted. On this subject, the institution today is at an impasse. Many fathers of the Church let their fantasies speak, and Rome has gone astray with this notion of perpetual virginity. How can we go back when we claim never to be wrong? How can we claim to be faithful to the Gospel and stifle its message? It is all the more tragic since the understanding of the mystery is largely lost as soon as we leave the symbolic field. With the advent of rationalist and scientific thought, we have impoverished our depth of understanding, which only now can be approached by an informed public.

Finally, it is a tragedy because women who have ceased to be absorbed in the Marian Dolorism (a philosophy that either exalts suffering or seeks to achieve a greater good through difficulty and pain) of past centuries have now had enough of this schizophrenic model of a virgin and mother and today prefer to leave the Church.

THE THEOLOGICAL MEANING OF MARY'S VIRGINITY

To avoid these dead ends, let us try to define what the theological meaning of Mary's virginity could be. Let us start with the central assertion of the first Christian authors: Jesus is both fully human, therefore born of a woman, and fully God, born outside of any sexual relationship. This formulation responds to a heretical current called Docetism (*dokein*, to appear), which has never really disappeared! Docetism considers the humanity of Jesus to be only an appearance. In short, it holds that he avoided living a full human life with its fears and sufferings. Authors confronted this heresy from the second century onward, Ignatius of Antioch reminded these heretics that Christ is "of the seed of David and of the Holy Spirit"; he is not a simple prophet, but the Messiah that Israel was waiting for. And to demonstrate this, the person of Mary is essential. She proves that Jesus "took flesh."

Theologian Donna Singles shows that, in order to oppose the Docetists, Irenaeus insisted on the fact that this is about the incarnation of a God in our world. Thus, "the virgin birth in Irenaeus is essentially a Christology, because it gives the key to the identity of Jesus, in the sense that it corresponds to the need for a savior who is not confined to the lineage of men born solely from the will of the flesh." In short, Mary's virginity "was necessary" to express the divinity of Jesus. But Donna Singles does not forget to say also that "thanks to Mary, Christ is not 'disguised as a man' as the Docetists wanted. A purely spiritual Christ, without real contact with our humanity, could not have done anything for us."[14] We can thus measure how much virginity is an important link in theological reasoning. It is therefore essential not to be mistaken when seeking to qualify it. And we go astray when we separate it from the one it designates, Jesus. Yet this is what we will begin to do from the third century onward, as we have just seen, by making it become an end in which we are interested for its own sake. The door is then opened to the concept of perpetual virginity, which prepares the way for the two recent dogmas.

The Gospel of John, however, evokes a different, totally symbolic birth, since it takes place at the mature age of a human being. Jesus is "born" in Cana, through the encouragement of his mother. This choice is prudent, because it allows us to avoid gynecological tropism, a source of mythological or irrational deviations.

To understand the virginal conception with a contemporary theological eye, let us follow the suggestions of the Jesuit Bernard Sesboüé. He no longer observes it from the incarnation but from the resurrection, stating that "it is faith in the Resurrection that makes possible faith in the virginal conception and not the opposite."[15] If we believe that Christ is resurrected, then it becomes easier to welcome this good news of the entry of the Word into the world. "The faith required, in this case for the Resurrection, is based on serious signs and testimonies, but radically exceeds the order of historical proof."[16]

If the coming of the Son of God into the world is of the same order as his resurrection, that is to say, without any constraints on our rationality, it is futile to reject the virginal conception of Jesus, even if this Christian mystery scandalizes human reason. The believing approach proposed by Bernard Sesboüé allows us to welcome this mystery without renouncing the correct understanding of the event on the christological level. However, the idea of perpetual virginity offers nothing to the content of faith and contravenes the examination of biblical texts, without any benefit for understanding who Jesus is for us.

This is broadly what Joseph Ratzinger wrote: "The doctrine of the divinity of Jesus would not be called into question if Jesus had been born of a normal marriage. Because the divine filiation of which faith speaks is not a biological fact..., it is situated in the eternity of God."[17]

Another contemporary theologian, Christian Duquoc, questioned this interest in Mary's virginity:

> Is there not an unconscious overestimation of sexuality? In short, are women not being excluded from ministerial function because of this unexpressed but ideally transposed overestimation? I wonder. And this questioning is all the more pressing because a second element works in the same direction: the refusal to confer ordination on married men.[18]

This questioning leads us to explore in more depth the background to and assumed links in the Catholic Church between virginity and sexuality more broadly, and the concept of purity.

FROM VIRGINITY TO THE EXALTATION OF PURITY

Virginity is not just virginity. It implies the absence of sexual relations and therefore of sexual pleasure. This is an important consequence that the Catholic Church has not failed to seize upon. We know how much the Church, losing its Jewish origins on this subject as on others, has cast a suspicion of impurity on all sexual relations since Antiquity. In doing so, she limited the place of pleasure to the strict need of procreation. If Mary procreates without sexual intercourse, she escapes pleasure. We must question the reality, often observed throughout history, of a male anxiety about female pleasure. As if it had to be denied, forbidden, or even made physically impossible. Clitoral excision, which is still practiced today, is an example. On the contrary, we would have expected Christianity to value mutual pleasure as the happy consequence of a covenant. But patriarchy does not reason in terms of the liberation and autonomy of women.

In addition to the notion of pleasure rejected by the institution, the amalgamation of virginity and purity has been invited into the debate. These associations, these very prejudices, are fraught with consequences. How did the magisterium not measure the danger of "disembodying" the mother of Christ to make her a hybrid being, barely human? For if it can be admitted as an act of faith that Mary conceived Jesus without sexual intercourse with a man, beyond any dimension of personal pleasure, it is important to preserve the total human nature of Christ and to grant him, for this, a birth identical to that of any human being. Library shelves are filled with works strangely intermingling theology and obstetrics. There is mention of the hymen of Mary that would not have been torn, of the absence of a placenta, and, above all, it is stipulated that there was no pain at the time of childbirth. Why this insistence? To find only this shaky explanation: It was necessary for Mary to be able to escape the misinterpreted divine sentence of the Book of Genesis: "In pain you shall bring forth children" (3:16).

What complications and errors are due to a dubious interpretation! We have already recalled Paul Beauchamp's demonstration about Eve: God's verdict on childbirth is presented as a blessing rather than a punishment.[19] Let us also recall that Augustine, a great connoisseur of women before his conversion and a great slayer of all pleasure afterward, would comment on this theme by postulating that having conceived the child without carnal pleasure, Mary had birthed him without pain: "In his omnipotence, could not the Creator assimilate the mother's breast to that of the earth which conceives without voluptuousness and gives birth without pain?"[20] *Sic*! We measure by this rapprochement between the earth—insensible, inert, dug up, plowed—and the feminine body, nevertheless created by God with clay and the spirit, the monstrous mental violence exercised against women. It is a form of servitude. Everything, or almost everything is said in this odious way of putting sexual pleasure and the pains of childbirth in tension. In short, no pleasure, no pain....And too much pleasure, a lot of pain. These remarks will, alas, taint the lives of women for many centuries.

The question then becomes less about how giving birth to a child would defile a woman than about connecting childbirth to what generally preceded it: the nubility of a young woman, therefore subject to menstruation, then to sexual intercourse, and possibly to the pleasure linked to it. The entire biological identity of a woman is thus questioned by these religious prejudices to be either put on trial or concealed.

But this way of interpreting the incarnation raises questions. Why would the coming of God into Creation, since God chose to take on human flesh, modify the usual process of life? Why, for example, would there be no pleasure for Mary in conceiving from the Spirit the announced child?

Let us observe the lexical field used by Luke. The angel "enters" Mary, asks her to "rejoice," after which "she was greatly troubled," and the angel reassures her: "Do not be afraid, Mary." This staging leads a few verses later to this observation by the young woman: "My spirit leaps for joy."

If we extract these expressions from the religious context in which they are stated, everything will lead the reader to think that this is a first successful sexual experience. But is that not precisely what it is? The Spirit makes Mary enjoy herself, and she is enlightened by what is happening to her. She will then bear her child like any woman who has been made pregnant. Art enthusiastically represents her in a state of pregnancy, and sculptures of the pregnant Virgin enjoyed popular fervor in France, Spain, and Portugal between the thirteenth and sixteenth centuries. But from the Council of Trent onward, these works were confiscated, hidden, or destroyed, as if, through them, Mary had become too "human." As if above all the exposure of her pregnancy objectified the sexual act that it is important to make people forget. The ethnologist Jean-Yves Loude[21] associates the disappearance of these representations with the logic of a discourse of exclusion developed by religious men at the expense of half of humanity. Indeed, the obsession of the clergy is to "disembody" Mary as much as possible, to compose an ideal figure of her in order to keep at a distance everything that the body, especially the female body, could, according to them, contain links with impurity, with sin, or even with evil; let us translate: sexuality.

This denial of the body forgets that it is in its holistic dimension—soul, body, and psyche together—that the human being is the image of God invited to choose the path of "resemblance." This rejection of Mary's humanity, and consequently of all healthy corporeality, betrays the significance of the incarnation of the Word.

Beyond the officially condemned female pleasure, menstrual blood has very often provoked a reaction of fear in male individuals to the point that the Book of Leviticus, in its list of abominations leading to death, puts incest, homosexuality, bestiality, and sexual intercourse during menstruation on the same level: "If a man lies with a woman having her sickness and uncovers her nakedness, he has laid bare her flow, and she has laid bare her flow of blood; both of them shall be cut off from their people" (Lev 20:18). Moreover, the same book had already declared: "When a woman has a discharge of blood that is her regular discharge from her body, she shall be in her impurity for seven days, and whoever touches her shall be unclean until the evening" (Lev 15:19).

The perception of the impurity of this blood could have disappeared had Christianity decided no longer to follow the prescriptions of Leviticus, but this was not the case. Pope Gregory the Great (sixth century) once replied to Augustine of Canterbury, a bishop of England: "Menstruation is not a sin....But if nature is upset to the point of appearing defiled outside of all human will, it must come from a fault."[22]

Therefore, the link between menstruation and fault having been established, it reaches all women, starting with Eve, to discredit them. Mary, alone, must be an exception. Has anyone asked whether she had been menstruating? If, in addition to this obvious "impurity" that constitutes menstrual blood, a woman does not protect herself from the sexual act, she defiles herself even more. *Exit* Mary, then, out of the marital bedroom, and definitively, as stipulated by the dogma of perpetual virginity! An interpretation that, as we have emphasized, would have been considered aberrant in the world in which Jesus lived.

WHY THIS INSISTENCE ON PURITY?

The insistence on the laws of purity is at odds with the attendance on the divine. In most religions, until today, male priests organize the conditions, rituals, and modalities by which the divine will manifest itself. Purity occupies a central place. However, Christianity was born by wanting to distance itself from this model for which the Jewish cult provided an opportunity. In the beginnings of Christianity, there were no priests but "elders," chosen from the community for their probity and their relational charisms. They were the ones who presided over worship. But around 250, a major turning point occurred: "priests" appeared, charged with a "sacerdotal" ministry, that is, invested with the power to communicate with the sacred, the place of the divine. There were probably some women who presided over the celebrations since councils at the end of Antiquity renewed the ban on women approaching the "sacred vessels," indirect proof that this did indeed exist.[23] But the priests ended up being only men. The people became "profane," which etymologically means "far from the sacred," and the conditions of their access were regulated. One can imagine that these prescriptions could be very diverse, whether they were linked to faults, transgressions, ethnic characteristics, or finally to physical qualities. In the case of Christianity, they were ethical and especially of a bodily nature.

As we have already recalled, the body was very quickly denigrated in Christianity. Under the influence of many "dualist" religious and philosophical currents, that is, ones that opposed the soul to the body, the soul was judged to be noble and hindered by carnal reality. The bodies of women especially were quickly considered to be the seat of particularly disturbing impurities. Among these realities of the female body, menstrual blood was considered a defilement incompatible with the approach of any sacred space. The reasoning that leads to this is complex. On the one hand, if ancient medicine struggled to explain menstrual blood, it clearly perceived that a link existed between this blood and the capacity to bear a child. The woman was thus, through her blood, the place of a new, fascinating creation, a sign of her power, but which occurred in a certain mystery. It is, *in fine*, the procreative capacity of women that would be in question. If the masculine wants to keep its affinity with the sacred for itself alone, it must distance itself from this power of the feminine, decree this blood "impure," and deny the relationship of the feminine to Creation, in order to protect the assimilation between its own physical strength and the power it draws from it, an association that brings it closer to the divine and imposes it in a role of domination.[24] We can imagine that for this reason, among others, Eve's capacity to create remained misunderstood by Christian commentators. To do this, it would have been necessary to go beyond the representations linked to blood: the blood of the wounded warrior, the blood of Abel that the earth drinks. Blood points toward death, and therefore toward fear. Certainly, there is the blood of the covenant, but also that of sacrifices, shed by the high priest in expiation of sins.

By denying blood its power of life, the prohibitions decreed by men deny the corporeality of women. However, the corporeality of the human being is at the heart of the Judeo-Christian message, because it contributes to creation. It is to be honored, to be respected in its diversity, but never to be denigrated. The Gospels show that Jesus enjoyed festive meals with his friends, willingly met people who came to him, put his saliva on the eyes of a blind man, even defied the official ritual impurities of Jewish law, as revealed, among other things, in the parable of the "good Samaritan." Moreover, touched by the woman with the hemorrhage, he did not reproach her when he discovered that she was impure in the eyes of the Law.

Totally human and totally divine, Christ came in the flesh to save this corporeality that constitutes the human person. This is the very meaning of his incarnation. Consequently, denigrating the body in Christianity is an aberration at all levels. Paul will even say in his First Letter to the Corinthians: "Do you not know that you are God's temple, and that God's Spirit dwells in you?" (1 Cor 3:16). Would not the body of Mary and of the women after her be the temple of God? Through Christ, all Christians become the place of his presence; each baptized person is elevated to the titles of priest, prophet, and king. And if the liturgy of the Eucharist is indeed "source and summit of the Christian life," it is because it celebrates the encounter of God with all people. In this sacrament, Jesus "incorporates" himself into the one who shares in his life, forever present in our singularity.

Are we far from Mary? No. Mary is not a goddess; she is the mother of Jesus. She offered her virginity to God to give birth to God's Son, to transmit to him the human part of his being, but as far as she is concerned, it is in her full humanity that she carried Christ and on the symbolic level that she guides us.

We have seen that the virgin of Israel is the one who preserves herself from idols. The Book of Revelation confirms this again when it mentions the one hundred and forty-four thousand faithful who passed through the great trial and "are virgins" (Rev 14:4). They did not let themselves be corrupted by the Beast; they remained faithful to God, within the covenant. Here again, it is a question of ethical purity, not of physiology: "And in their mouth no lie was found; they are blameless" (Rev 14:5). Virginity belongs to the same symbolic register as the number of the chosen mentioned. Since this virginity is referred to in the metaphorical dimension and in the realm of faith, the question remains now of the content of Mary's motherhood, which has had such an impact on the lives of women for generations.

4

A UNIQUE MOTHERHOOD

WITHIN OUR QUESTIONING of the titles and roles imposed upon the figure of Mary, let us try to define the silhouette that the Gospels give us regarding her most referenced characteristic: her motherhood. How can we understand it? It is paradoxical that Mary has been considered the model of the mother, even when her motherhood, as we will rediscover together, is unique. We must redefine it from top to bottom, to compare its similarities and its differences to ordinary motherhood. Our investigation is just beginning.

The first impression that emerges from these Gospel stories is the profound distinctiveness of this motherhood. In a somewhat polemical way, the Asian scholar Ariane Buisset underlines what, according to the fathers of the Church, distinguished Mary from other women. The latter see her as an accomplished woman, but is she still what we would commonly call a woman? Buisset says,

> Their compliments to the Virgin will often emphasize that there was nothing feminine in her....The Christian paradox regarding femininity is stated thus: the woman worthy of the name has neither breasts, nor sex, nor generic form, and she has rejected everything that followed from them. She is not a man, she is not yet worthy of it, but she will soon become one, if she

> deserves it. This will be granted to her in paradise, if she is patient with her troubles, and if she fulfills her role as reproducer and servant on earth for her husband.[1]

This acerbic expression is a response to those ecclesiastics who, not content to reduce those women living outside convents to their maternal function, have given as a model of the ideal woman this unattainable paradigm: a virgin mother. This is the first chink in the halo of "exemplary mother" that crowns Mary. How could we not vigorously refuse to compare this unique motherhood to that experienced by ordinary women?

Whatever view one takes of the Gospel, and a fortiori if we accept the virginal conception, Mary is not a mother like any other. Any comparison in this sense is intolerable because it places women before a contradictory injunction. Since no woman can honor both terms, all become eternal culprits. And when they choose one or the other, virginity or the sexual life that eventually leads to motherhood, they will live in regret for a lost model. Thus, not only is the figure of Mary not the model of "the woman," but neither is she that of "the mother." Let us therefore accept, at the beginning of this chapter, the profound singularity of Mary's motherhood.

To progress with our research, let us question the primary witness of this extraordinary motherhood, Jesus. He never denies his humanity; he assumes the natural commonalities that make him the "son of Mary." But what he teaches us about his mother is both surprising and essential. From the beginning of his public mission, he categorically, and on several occasions, refused all ties that would hinder his mission, in particular family ties, and first of all the one that connects him to his mother: "'Who are my mother and my brothers?' And looking around at those who sat around him, he said, 'Here are my mother and my brothers! Whoever does the will of God is my brother and sister and mother'" (Mark 3:33–34). And also: "Whoever comes to me and does not hate father and mother, wife and children, brothers and sisters, yes, and even life itself, cannot be my disciple" (Luke 14:26).

Jesus even considers the hypothesis that the breakup of the family unit might be necessary to follow him, and he assumes it with determination at the risk of undermining his audience:

> Do you think that I have come to bring peace to the earth? No, I tell you, but rather division! From now on, five in one household will be divided, three against two and two against three; they will be divided father against son and son against father, mother against daughter and daughter against mother, mother-in-law against her daughter-in-law and daughter-in-law against mother-in-law. (Luke 12:51–53)

Through these words, Jesus does not seek to reject his birth, nor to question motherhood or family values, but he establishes a social motherhood and fraternity much broader than those of blood. Therein lies fecundity, that is to say, the result, the fruit. In fact, Jesus promises a fertility much more fruitful than that of simple blood ties: "Truly, I tell you, there is no one who has left house or wife or brothers or parents or children for the sake of the kingdom of God, who will not get back very much more in this age, and in the age to come eternal life" (Luke 18:29–30).

A MOTHERHOOD WITH SYMBOLIC CONNOTATIONS TOO

Let us ask ourselves for a moment how Mary could have understood such words, if deep interior work had not pushed her toward a radical conversion. In fact, what remains of motherhood if it is severed from what, in the common understanding, creates it? What becomes of the notions of resemblance, of a privileged bond, of boundless affection, of social honorability between the mother and her child, at a time when women were recognized only if they became mothers? In fact, Mary does not renounce them without effort. When Jesus is twelve years old, and the family returns to Nazareth after a pilgrimage to Jerusalem, she reproaches her son for having stayed there and left them in anguish. Jesus answers her that he must be in the temple, in his Father's house (see Luke 2:41–50). A hard word for Mary to hear. Within her, the mother of the child and the mother of the Christ who must be left to his mission undoubtedly intersect and clash.

But this distance established by Jesus is also an advantage. He designates a new place for her, that of a disciple. He invites her to follow the program, the same teaching that he will propose to his companions: to do the will of the Father, to work for the kingdom. And, as Georgette Blaquière notes, this proposal is an achievement:

> Do we really appreciate the space of freedom that these words open up to the modern woman as well as to the Jewish woman, when she, too, is called as a free person to follow Christ, and this call transcends the bonds of a child with his mother and of a mother with her child? The early Church understood this well..., it opens the way to a true liberation of the woman by seeing her as an autonomous person, and not only as a wife and potential mother.[2]

By embracing the vocation of every disciple, Mary, without seeing her legitimate emotional ties disappear, is now freed from the rigid behavioral models to which the functions of wife and mother can lead: possessiveness, authoritarianism, and at the same time, the resignation of any other responsibility than that linked to her motherhood.

Jesus is perhaps the first in Western history to offer women a vocation outside of their motherhood. We must take note of this liberation, especially when we compare it to the gendered assignments of the Catholic institution. What a shame that the latter is not aware, on the one hand, of its infidelity to the message of Christ, and on the other hand, of the limitation it imposes on women by continuing to value virginity or motherhood as the only accomplishments offered to them. John Paul II and Benedict XVI persisted in affirming that the dignity of "the" woman comes from the Marian model, an exclusively maternal model, and they always maintained the parallel between Eve and the submissive and obedient holy woman that Mary was for them.

These multiple roles are not only detrimental to women. They also affect men who cannot relate to a model of a woman who will never be anything other than wife and mother. So, what is left for us that can be modelled in Mary's motherhood?

When Mary Fed the Saints with Her Milk

The maternal figure of Mary has served as a basis for scenes that are sometimes a thousand miles from the Gospels. The pictorial representation known as the "Lactation of Saint Bernard" is an example of the extravagances, and even the delirium, that can result from distance from the Gospel stories. The great reformer of the Cistercian order is said to have received Mary's milk in a vision. This theme was born in the Middle Ages but became famous at the time of the Catholic Reformation when it was necessary to reaffirm the maternal and tender proximity of the mother of God. Painters took up the subject and treated it in various ways. While all show the saint in ecstasy receiving Mary's milk, some, for example, omit the baby Jesus from the painting. Others introduce a character who symbolizes the spectator, who is forced to enter the scene and experience it too.

One of the best-known paintings is that of Alonzo Cano. The scene takes place in a church. The baby Jesus is in his mother's arms and, astonished, follows with his eyes the powerful jet of milk that crosses the space, until it lands in the open mouth of the saint, who kneels in the church in front of the altar. But the work that raises the most questions is undoubtedly that of Juan Simon Gutierrez, who portrays Saint Dominic about to be breastfed by Mary. We see the saint in ecstasy, eyes half-closed, lying on the knees of Mary who embraces him with her left arm and, with her right arm, prepares to open her garment, which is red, to free her breast and offer it to him. Mary and the saint are surrounded by a hillside of young women saints each holding the palm of martyrdom. Lactation is attested by the title given to the work, but it is more suggested than shown. On the other hand, the physical enjoyment of the saint, face turned upside down, eyes half-closed, is obvious.

The usual interpretations of this scene are that Mary's milk opens the way to the milk of the scriptures, and therefore to the knowledge of God, or that Mary is the mother of humanity, which must be educated by her milk, that is, by her example as a generous mother. Today, it is easy to discount these practices on the grounds of our knowledge of the psychic mechanisms that govern the human being. Clearly, in this motif, the saint takes Mary for his mother, and he projects all his feelings onto her. In the case of Saint Dominic, the relationship takes on incestuous connotations. Perhaps the audacity of this scene allowed the painters or the patrons to resolve certain internal conflicts? But how can faith accommodate such a gap with the biblical record? Mary of the Gospels is more than a physical mother with whom to engage in a kind of therapy. She is there to point to her son, and when he is missing, everything is missing.

MARY, A TRUE WOMAN OF ISRAEL

In order to identify the unique maternity of Mary, it is useful to devote a few lines to verifying how Mary, assuming her Jewishness, is deeply linked to Israel. As Schalom Ben-Chorin writes in his book *Mary: A Jewish Look at the Mother of Jesus*, it is important to lay bare "the Jewish face of a young mother from Galilee."[3]

Mary belongs to the Jewish people, and nothing should distinguish her a priori from the women of her country. She bears the most banal first name in Israel, Myriam; she has nothing of the illustrious figures of its history, like Sarah, Deborah, or Judith. She could be "the poor Jewess of Judea," according to Péguy's words.[4] However, from reading Matthew's genealogy, we guess that her destiny will be extraordinary. She is preceded by four women,[5] all of whom, Jewish or not, break with the social order of their time. Energetic and determined, they listen to the Spirit who pushes them to accept improbable choices. Through their transgressions, they contribute to transmitting the faith of Israel and to founding this composite and strong people. Mary is from this family.

Her position as a Jewish woman is inscribed from the beginning of the Gospel of Luke in the lines of the longest text put on the lips of a woman in the New Testament, the Magnificat, where Luke describes her as a true daughter of Abraham, anchored in the faith of her people. She will accomplish what had been announced. The echoes in this programmatic text of a song from the First Testament, the song of Hannah, indelibly inscribes her in the history of the people of God, to lead them toward the new covenant (see 1 Sam 2:1–10). Mary participates in the fulfillment of the scriptures by accepting a unique place, that of mother of the Messiah; therefore, a Jewish mother.

This anchoring in Israel is also illustrated by the parallel that exists between Mary's declaration to the angel—"Let it be with me according to your word" (Luke 1:38)—and the people's response to Moses: "All that the Lord has spoken we will do, and we will be obedient" (Exod 24:7). In both cases, the action precedes the formulation. It happens first, then it is explained; this is the characteristic of the movement of Israel.

We have noticed that Mary's virginity speaks of the disposition of the heart to remain faithful to the covenant, and that the emphasis is placed on her role as mother. It is as a future mother that she vibrated with joy at the announcement of the child; it is for the life of this child that she imposes her pregnancy on Joseph and assumes precarious living conditions, both material and social. We must understand, from reading the Gospels, that Mary was for Jesus as any Jewish woman had to be at that time for her child. She had her son circumcised; she taught him the Torah that she knows perfectly, as the weaving of biblical references that is in her Magnificat invites us to understand. The Gospel also shows us how she put herself in danger for her son, from the annunciation until her presence at the cross and in the Upper Room while the followers of this "troublemaker" Jesus feared being hunted. Therefore, like his mother, Jesus is Jewish, born into the Jewish people, living according to the Jewish law that he comes to universalize without ever denying his heritage.

The wedding at Cana, the place of the first "sign" of Jesus in the Gospel of John (see John 2:1–11), depicts a form of motherhood that differs from that described in the infancy narratives. Mary's faith in her son is based on more than her love as a mother, since it has been announced to her that her Jesus, "the Messiah," will be great, that he will be the Son of God, heir to the throne of David, and that his reign will have no end (see Luke 1:32). Her confidence incites her to bring about the revelation of her son by almost conceiving a sort of new "birth" that gives birth to Jesus as sent by God. By showing a less passive, less retiring face, Mary is not less a mother, nor does she suppress the other.

At his moment of giving life, Jesus makes Mary the mother of the beloved disciple and makes the disciple the son of Mary (see John 19:26). In this way, Jesus integrates the whole community into the heart of this new birth. We all become brothers and sisters through Mary, from whom Jesus detaches himself by calling her "woman." This surprising and symbolic denomination marks a distancing between our humanity and his divinity. It does not disqualify Mary's motherhood but refers well beyond it. Already, the Book of Genesis had announced that "the woman" would crush evil by referring to the first woman: Eve. The same word now designates Mary, who allows the message of Christ, intended for all, to sink its roots in the history and the Law of the chosen people. In this, Mary is indeed the "Jewish mother" who brings with her the heritage of her people, now proposed to all readers of the Gospels. At the same time, the term *woman* prepares the universalization that goes beyond Mary's Jewishness.

But Mary's motherhood exceeds that of a woman who carries with her the history of God's chosen people. She is also the *theotokos*, "Mother of God," or more literally, his genetrix. This decision of the Council of Ephesus in 431 ended up verifying popular veneration and proving Cyril, the Bishop of Alexandria, right against Nestorius, Archbishop of Constantinople, who found it sufficient to call her *christotokos*, "Mother of the Christ."

Following this council, which greatly challenged the theologians of the time, it would be necessary to wait another twenty years and for another council, that of Chalcedon, in 451, to see this affirmation through to the end. Indeed, that this maternity is divine again questions the identity of Jesus. What do the acts of this council say when they affirm that Jesus is "true God and true man at the same time, without confusion or change"? The debates were lively, and serious explanations were necessary to show that the existence of the Son of God born of Mary did not begin in her. However, no one among the council fathers contested that the Word was made flesh in Mary, in the heart of the people of God, the Jewish people, and that as such, Mary is a woman of a different quality from all other women, without it being imaginable to imitate her, since no other has been chosen by God to bear the Messiah.

Thus, in questioning Mary's motherhood, we have noted a discreet disturbance in its current understanding. One by one, the many unique qualities of this motherhood have appeared. Above all, we have rediscovered how the main actor in this displacement is Jesus himself, who dismisses Mary from the privileges usually associated with motherhood, to propose that she be a disciple among others. We conclude from this investigation that Mary's motherhood, comparable to no other, cannot be proposed as a model to women. It must be understood in the symbolic register, both because it is inimitable and because it concerns all believers. Its reason for being is to signify the greatness of the Son thus engendered, the Messiah.

Part 2
THE EVIDENCE

NOW THAT WE have freed Mary from her patriarchal and clerical burden, do we know her better? It is still too early. We will only really understand her after having gathered the evidence of our investigation. Now, instead of a counterfeit figure deprived of her body and her dynamism, disinvested then reinvested to serve political interests, the figure of Mary that we have promised you cannot disappoint, because she carries within her the overall promise of the evangelical message. Mary, the mother of Jesus, cannot be the one who imposes a destiny of submission on women. She cannot lock believers into dead ends. She can only free believers from them and refer each one to the greatness of their vocation. Mother of the Savior, she can only hold open the door that leads to salvation. We will therefore in this second part, example after example, piece by piece, bring together all the components of the "Mary of the Gospels."

In two chapters, we will first undertake a biblical journey without taboos, highlighting several women whose story joins or echoes that of Mary. Then, in two other chapters, we will detail the work of Luke, poetically called "the painter of the Virgin," for his two paintings of inexhaustible richness, that of the annunciation and that of the Magnificat. This will allow us afterward, in the third and final part of this work, to draw as faithfully as possible the portrait of the one who brought Jesus into the world.

5

A LITTLE BIBLICAL INVESTIGATION

DISCOURSE ON MARY must start from scripture, not from theology, because she cannot be found nor faith in her justified without recourse to it. Certainly, tradition and the familial heritage of believers, whether they come from the teachings of the Church or from popular practices, have their place, but only on condition that they refer back to scripture. It is this which puts the "sense" in the Christian spiritual approach that we call the *sensus fidei* or sense of faith. Because, if it is by faith that a believer knows Mary, that person will return to biblical sources to avoid making a pact with idolatry by divinizing Mary. In the absence of this solid anchoring, shifts in meaning and representations can betray the message, all the more surely since the small number of sources and the few testimonies from the first communities encourage us to fill in the blanks in the text. We have already seen the harm that this does.

If, in pursuing our investigation, we turn to the Bible, let us first dismiss the prejudice according to which the New Testament tells us so little about Mary that she becomes a difficult figure to elucidate. We will soon verify this. To know Mary, we must make a detour through the great female figures of the First Testament who occupied the Jewish cultural universe, the landscape of the biblical writers. Indeed, among the female biblical characters, Mary has older sisters.

This is why we must look for what were the tutelary figures of the New Testament writers and, first, answer two questions.

How did they think of women? How did male commentators report their presence?

IS THE BIBLICAL UNIVERSE HOSTILE TO WOMEN?

When we read the Bible closely, we see that women have a completely different place in it than that which has been taught by traditional piety and constructed by male commentators. Until the decades following the Second Vatican Council, biblical teachings were transmitted exclusively by single men whose feminine reference was generally their own mother, sometimes their sister. No need for long psychoanalytic studies to measure the influence that this can have on the way we consider the female characters of the scriptures, even if history offers some beautiful exceptions, such as that of the Cappadocian father of the fifth century, Basil of Caesarea, who, thanks to the teaching of his sister, Macrina, proposed a more enlightened approach to the place of women. Today, many exegetes are women. And when they are men, they open the door to a rereading of the Bible that better integrates the presence of women.

Should we, however, take it for granted that the biblical patriarchal universe was hostile to women? The answer to this question is more nuanced than we sometimes hear. The environment in which Jesus lived, like that which preceded him, was not this macho world that certain modern currents imagine. Certainly, we are in patriarchal times in which physical strength prevails, as much for waging war as for cultivating the fields. The ancient separation between the public and domestic spheres is therefore quite clear, but we will soon see that in Israel, it is less so than elsewhere.

If the priority place of Jewish women remains the private domain, which does not prevent them from knowing the scriptures, it is necessary to recall the significant value that was their responsibility, that of the *toledôth*, the succession of generations.

We see, for example, in the lives of the matriarchs Sarah, Rebecca, Leah, and Rachel, how sterility and fertility are at the center of women's lives, sometimes at the cost of jealousies and terrible quarrels, as between Jacob's two wives, Leah and Rachel (see Gen 29:15–30). This importance given to procreation will be translated by the law of levirate marriage, which encourages every widow to marry her brother-in-law. Even if the point of this law aims to give descendants to the husband, it nevertheless turns out to be a protection for women, who most often are thereby assured of not remaining without resources and defenseless in their widowhood.

Faced with the harshness of the times, marked by wars, diseases, famines, of which some biblical books bear traces (see 1 Kgs 17:8–16), Israel responded with a war of the cradles. A numerically tiny people, it had to grow in order to try to carry weight in the concert of nations. The honors that, as a result, surrounded motherhood attenuated male domination. Of course, other signs of patriarchy emerge here and there in the many prescriptions that punctuate life. In this highly codified society, tradition indicated that a woman had less value than a man, and it illustrated this in a way that seems unbearable today. Thus, to honor an important personage or to show hospitality toward a stranger, it was possible to propose one's daughter for a sexual relationship: "Here is my virgin daughter...do whatever you want" (Judg 19:24). However, a young girl who was raped, becoming unfit for marriage, generally ended up killed.

Despite everything, the Bible insists that men and women come from the same flesh, that of the primordial Adam. Leviticus does not fail to remind us of this to justify sexual prohibitions: "they are your flesh" (Lev 18:17). And above all, the Bible takes its concerns further. It places men and women under the gaze of God, to remind them that God does not endorse these divisions but transcends them. God does not speak in force, in thunder, but through the little ones, the forgotten, the meek, the excluded. In this reversal of values, three categories are clearly identified in the First Testament: the poor of the Lord called the *anawim*, the foreigners, and the women. Thus, the Book of Judith[1] shows how "the Almighty has foiled them by the hand of a woman" (Jdt 16: 5).

In many biblical episodes, women are given as examples for having acted according to God's heart. But from this major observation, let us not deduce that God considers women as superior beings by nature. The equality of all remains the guiding principle. God values certain gendered attitudes such as gentleness, discretion, and interiority, of which women are the representatives in the Jewish culture of the time, but God also exalts moral strength, the refusal of servile submission, the taste for freedom demonstrated by true heroines such as Deborah, Tamar, Esther, Ruth, and Judith. All these qualities are the common heritage of humanity, offered to all, men and women. If the Bible recalls the equality of all, it can only do so within the patriarchal frameworks that prevailed at the time. This is why we must avoid the anachronism that overvalues certain attitudes. Furthermore, the Church has firmly recalled that scripture must be placed in its context and that prescriptions that no longer have any place must be set aside.[2] This is the case with the codes of laws in Leviticus, for example.

In the name of this fundamental equality, the Bible condemns the violence that has often been practiced against women. An example illustrates the horror of this violence. In chapter 19 of the Book of Judges, an old man, in order not to fail in his sense of hospitality, offers his virgin daughter to the men of the tribe of Benjamin who want to force him to chase away the traveler he was hosting. It is finally the guest's concubine who is handed over to them. These men abuse her all night and in the morning leave her for dead. Mad with grief, the visitor cuts the concubine into twelve pieces, as many as there are tribes in Israel, and sends one piece to each of the twelve tribes. While the biblical writer tells this story to condemn the perpetrators of this crime, the violence of this text leaves one speechless and reminds us of the danger of any fundamentalist reading.

THE PITFALLS OF A PATRIARCHAL INTERPRETATION

To fully appreciate the importance of equality between men and women affirmed by the Bible, we must look at the two creation stories in the Book of Genesis. While it is easy to verify that, in the first story, on the sixth day, God creates man and woman together and does not treat them any differently (Gen 1:26–27), the matter seems more nuanced in the second story. But before examining it, let us recall in broad outline how it unfolds.

We all believe we know this verse well, which we read most often in translation as: "The Lord God said: 'It is not good that the man should be alone" (Gen 2:18). But the Hebrew says something else: "It is not good that the man [*ha 'adâm*, not "man" in the masculine sense] should be alone." The Hebrew word used in this verse is the same as that used in the first creation story to designate humanity; ambiguity is therefore impossible. The result of this rectification, apparently minimal compared to common readings, is, in reality, considerable. It dismisses the male from a claim that he has nevertheless made for several millennia, by endorsing the idea that "man" and "humanity" would be identical. We must measure the immense consequences of this masculine coup de force. How many works of art show us a male installed in front of the Creator, who extracts from one of his ribs a tiny, still-wrinkled woman? Even Michelangelo was caught out when, on the ceiling of the Sistine Chapel, he painted the hand of God touching a virile being to give him life. In this matter as in others, art has been the revealer of everyday life in the West for twenty centuries: It shows us, by their absence, that the existence of women is not recognized and that their word does not count. Invisibility to the point of denial.

The story then informs us that this human being is suffering, that he will have to be saved from solitude. To remedy this, the Creator says: "I want to make him an '*ezer*,'" which is generally translated as "helper." God therefore sends upon the human "a deep sleep" that leaves the human with no memory.

Now, as we have shown[3] and as many contemporary exegetes confirm,[4] everywhere else this word *ezer* means "rescuer." One scholar, André Wénin,[5] recalls that the word *rescuer* is precise in biblical Hebrew; it always refers to the intervention of God to save a life from mortal peril. In this verse, it can only contain this meaning. We then guess that this divine prerogative of "rescuing" will now be given to humanity; it will come about when two new beings are placed face-to-face from the primordial being. Let us observe that this "rescue" is not "matched" to the first like an object that would be well suited. "It" is a subject. In other words, from this "re-creation" are born two different human beings in a situation of otherness who discover each other "face-to-face." Thus, in a few words, this verse teaches the imperative of a relationship that is neither vertical as between God and God's creatures, nor an extension of a "same," but strong in the richness of a recognition of a different other.

Creation is therefore composed of a humanity marked by a face-to-face encounter (they are two, equal and different), and this second chapter of Genesis confirms the first message of Genesis (1:27) that denies any possibility of subordination of one by the other. Humanity is inaugurated with a call to life that was impossible for it in the solitude of this primordial being, made of the clay of the ground.

Yet, a completely different teaching has been transmitted by the ecclesiastical institution. As we have just noted, according to Catholic tradition, the masculine man represents humanity, and the woman, without needing to be cited, is included in it. This bias that has guided Western thought for almost two millennia was studied for the first time in 1903 by the American sociologist Lester Frank Ward, who gave it the name "androcentrism." The term was taken up decades later, in 1976, by theologian Kari Elisabeth Børresen in an article in the journal *Concilium.* She defined it as a doctrine of the relationship between man and woman developed from the sole point of view of man, without any intention of reciprocity.

The Bible shows us that God, the All Other, has no gender. God created two human beings face-to-face, male and female, while preserving their original specificity: that of a primordial being created in God's image. Everything will therefore not be expressed by biological characteristics, unlike in the animal kingdom. And above all, it is *together*, man *and* woman, that the human is in the image of God. What consequences this little conjunction of "coordination" has! It is only in respect, cooperation, connection, and mutual concern that man and woman access the image. Isolated, one without the other, they deprive themselves of it.

On a broader level, another theologian, Elisabeth Moltmann-

Wendel, was one of the first to reread the history of women in the Bible, ridding it of clerical distortions. She shows that such figures as Sarah, Deborah, and Jael are clear signs of an ancient feminine culture.[6] She also sees in the first Christian assemblies the reflection of a privileged status of women, contrary to the surrounding world.

Thus, in the Bible, the many women presented are sometimes wives, like Sarah or Zippora, who encourage, stimulate, or even guide the mission of their husbands, sometimes women who receive a direct charge to come to the aid of the community and find in themselves, in their commitment and their faith, their sense of duty. Sometimes women oppose unacceptable orders from their husbands. Thus, the wife of King Ahasuerus, Vashti, refused to dance naked before a group of courtiers, and she was repudiated (Esth 1:9–22) for her disobedience. Who, today, would blame her? All these women, Jewish or foreign, will be the links that prepare for the coming of Christ. That they use the most controversial resources of their femininity, such as Judith, who seduces Holofernes, or Esther, who, from the depths of her harem, devoted twelve months of her life to preparing her body with oils and ointments before presenting herself before the king (Esth 2:12–14), does not prevent them from becoming instruments of God. Puritans, abstain....

All these women, whom traditional holy history has made so little of, are, in reality, strangely present. They show that Israel can lend itself to listening to extraordinary messages. They will remain so when the Word becomes flesh. But patriarchal power has too often concealed the place of women in scripture. Today, important parts of the history of Israel are being reconstituted because we agree to take into account the part of women in the history of salvation. As for the figure of Mary, it is the same. Her story is enriched by that of the great figures of the First Testament. It is therefore necessary for us to take an interest in them.

EVE, AGAIN

The reason for this journey back in time is to reveal the interplay of connections in the analysis of the scriptures and the affinities that exist between certain figures and Mary. We can thus affirm that Mary has "older sisters" in the First Testament. The biblical writers know very well, by a simple allusion, how to connect a figure to other older ones that have already expressed something that is consonant with what they want to say. They "summon" other behaviors, other commitments, that the final figure can then claim. Some of the information we need about Mary has already been provided earlier, in other portraits.

From this perspective, we must begin by looking with new eyes at the relationship between the first two human beings of Genesis. We will see how their relationship was biased in the direction of male domination that will hinder dialogue, which will not happen between Mary and her son.

We know that in chapter 3 of Genesis, just after the pronouncement of the sentences that follow the "fall," the woman is named "Eve" by her spouse, recognizing her characteristic of being "mother of all who live" (Gen 3:20). The name of Adam (*Adâm*), as the male element opposite, is mentioned in chapter 4 when he acquires his full recognition as the genitor by the conception of Seth (see Gen 4:25). We can easily hear the similarity of this name with the designation of *ha 'adâm* who was the first nongendered human being. Hence the risk of amalgamating the generic human of the initial creation with the male who faces the woman.

The ambiguity is maintained even in the New Testament when Paul speaks of the "transgression of Adam" in his Letter to the Romans. It is therefore necessary to emphasize the flow of the interpretation. Long centuries of catechesis have maintained that the feminine had been created from the "male Adam" and that the woman was subordinate to him. In addition, "disobedient Eve–Adam first male" found expression in the new tandem Mary the "new Eve" and Christ the "new Adam." We have amply shown that this parallel is inexact since Christ, the "new Adam" of whom Paul speaks (Rom 5:12–21), is not "the new male" but the whole of humanity. His masculinity is only circumstantial in the process of an incarnation that aims at universality. It is the humanity of Christ that counts, and not his sex, which he never mentions as an element that would enhance or discredit a part of the human species. In this, Christ is "the Word" of God and therefore constitutes one of the Trinity. But neither Eve, in the couple that binds her to Adam, nor Mary in relation to Christ, must be disqualified. They, two women, are nevertheless the first victims of these shifts in meaning orchestrated around a sexualization that, little by little, will discount all women. Eve, created second from a modest rib taken from man, as if he were almost her progenitor, will be judged subordinate, the "second sex." Mary, so submissive to her Son, is made silent by history.

There is another point of similarity between Eve and Mary: their capacity for initiative. By observing how each of them uses their faculties of speech and communication, we will show how Mary reoriented the meaning of dialogue.

Eve is the one who dares to converse, first with the serpent, then with God, seeking to understand her environment. However, the first man and the first woman do not speak to each other, and even less do they respond to each other, especially the man, who exclaims: "This at last is bone of my bones and flesh of my flesh" (Gen 2:23). Contrary to what Georgette Blaquière writes on this subject, the man's first word in no way resembles a cry of love for his wife.[7] This is not a broadening of his horizons either, since he recognizes neither the otherness that has just been presented, nor the imperative of alliance. On the contrary, this brand-new man already claims ownership of what is detached from the primordial Adam. He shamelessly uses the possessive: "*my* bones," "*my* flesh." André Wénin points out that "outside of him, woman is still a kind of object—a fulfilling object that he claims belongs to him (bone of my bones and flesh of my flesh)—without even mentioning the divine handiwork."[8]

Does the figure of Mary have a role in this comparison? Mary, like Eve, dares to take the initiative. John describes this very well in the way she solicits her son during the wedding at Cana. We will see, by analyzing this scene for itself, how Mary, unlike Eve, enters into dialogue with Jesus, obtains his response, which will be first to reject her proposal, then to fulfill it and thus accomplish his first miracle. The cooperation that the first woman in the Bible was unable to obtain, due to the possessive incomprehension of her partner, finds its resolution in Mary's relationship with Jesus and leads him to reveal his mission. What a beautiful progression from the Old to the New Testament!

SARAH AND MARY, TWO LIVES EXPOSED

Let us move forward in the biblical story. Another comparison is necessary that further anchors the mother of Jesus in the people of Israel: that of her link with the wife of Abraham,[9] the matriarch Sarah. Eve and Mary have in common the fact of being "mothers." If Mary, on the symbolic level, can be called "mother of believers," renewing the image of Eve as "mother of the living," Sarah can be called "mother of the chosen people," evoking even greater richness.

Let us observe Sarah and Mary in their environments and compare their roles in a patriarchal context. Sarah's story is rich in lessons, but it begins badly: The narrator tells us that Sarah is sterile (Gen 11:30), and her story begins with a lie (Gen 12:11–20). Indeed, just before the couple, driven to Egypt by famine, are presented to Pharaoh, Abraham, fearing he will be killed, asks Sarah to say that she is his sister and not his wife. Sarah consents and will therefore be subjected to Pharaoh's predation. It is in this context that we encounter the first exchange in the Bible between a man and a woman. What a strange example of complicity is this lie to which Sarah consents, at the price of a possible rape for the salvation of her husband! The story of Mary also begins badly: The young girl risks stoning when she agrees to lose her virginity before her wedding and therefore to become a mother without having a husband. According to Matthew, the risk is real; it is clearly said that Joseph seeks to repudiate her quietly (Matt 1:19). In both cases, these women risk their lives, and they do it knowingly.

What, then, does a comparison between Sarah and the mother of Jesus suggest? As we have seen, Sarah's position with Abraham is neither assured nor valued. She must cheat on her social status and risk her physical integrity to save her husband's life. Then, faced with the ordeal of sterility, she will suggest to him to have a child through their servant Hagar. Later, finally the mother of Isaac, she will doubtless believe she is losing him when Abraham considers sacrificing him. However, Sarah remains firm in her faith, as she remains firm in the support of a husband who does not always choose the clearest or easiest solutions. Even so, these moral accommodations of the "Father of believers" do not prevent the great veneration of his tomb as well as that of Sarah in the city of Hebron.

Thus, Sarah's infertility, then her fertility at an age that defies biology, are two factors of precariousness comparable to Mary's pregnancy and childbirth. Two unique motherhoods...

Matthew and Luke, in their own way, show us that Mary transgresses, as Sarah had also transgressed. Both do it "for God," and their attitude shows that nothing can be done without the hand of their Lord. Being pregnant at almost one hundred years old, or being pregnant without a husband, is almost the same thing. Both women benefit from a divine election; both are vectors of the covenant.

As for the Fourth Gospel, it paints Mary with traits that are not unlike those that the First Testament gives to Abraham's wife. John, when he recounts the episode of Cana, gives Mary a determination similar to that of Sarah who, in order to preserve the inheritance of her son Isaac, repudiates Hagar and her son Ishmael (Gen 21:8–21). Sarah's firm decision has the consequence of asserting the rights of Isaac, "the child of the promise" made by God, and with him, those of the "chosen people." At Cana, Mary hastens the revelation of the hour of Jesus (see John 2:4), which gives rise to the first sign of his divinity. Sarah and Mary therefore act with the authority of the "matriarchs" who uphold the values of the people of Israel and want to guarantee their greatness for all time.

If we accept this kinship between the two women, we arrive at a portrait very different from that painted by the fathers, focused on the opposition between Eve and Mary that they had constructed. Far from opposing each other, Sarah and Mary show an obvious continuity. They are neither obedient nor submissive to the established order. Both demonstrate autonomy and clairvoyance: Sarah before Pharaoh and Hagar, Mary by her acquiescence to the angel and by the impetus that she gives to her son at Cana.

Both experience motherhoods decisive for humanity. Indeed, it is through the maternity of Sarah, who adheres to God's plan for Abraham to make him the "father of a multitude," that the eternal alliance between God and God's people is established. Similarly, Mary pronounces without hesitation her yes that will save humanity and renew the covenant by welcoming into her womb the Word of God as Sarah received in her womb the fruit of the promise. Both, as Paul noted regarding Sarah (see Gal 4:22–26), demonstrate absolute freedom. Nothing encumbers them when it is a question of serving God.

Scripture also reveals the firmness they show in dangerous situations. Sarah stops at nothing to bear the child who will fulfill the promise and open the way for the people as numerous as the stars (Gen 15:5), who will come with her and through her. She sets in motion the process that Mary will continue.

Through these two women, "communion in an unconditional attachment to Christ was sealed. It is a form of fulfillment of the scriptures which is then realized."[10] Sarah initiates; Mary responds.

Finally, the two women have in common the strength and courage of a powerful language. We will soon see that, in the Magnificat (Luke 1:46–56), Mary's strength is one of the first traits that appears. Mary celebrates the God of the covenant "in favor of Abraham and his descendants forever." Moreover, it is verified here that, for Luke, Mary is truly a daughter of Abraham and Sarah, anchored in the faith of her people to lead them toward the new covenant.

Yet, to our great surprise, this connection between the first of the matriarchs and the mother of Jesus has been little explored until recent years. Could it be because it highlights characteristics incompatible with those that the ecclesiastics value in their female portraits? Would it be painful for the clergy to recognize that Mary and Sarah are similar? Is it not apparent that Sarah is clairvoyant and complicit with her husband, that she does not disavow him before Pharaoh, and that she never places herself in a position of subordination? On the contrary, everything in their relationship manifests their love, their equality, and their solidarity with the aim of bringing about God's plan. How can we not see that Mary has the same determination, a natural complicity with Joseph, the same freedom with regard to established rules, that she stops at nothing to bring about the new covenant?

The difficulty for a patriarchal institution would perhaps be to admit—apart from the fact that the patriarch Abraham did not behave in a glorious way—that the two women let God guide the future of their sons, whatever suffering it cost them. Sarah will never see Isaac again after his ascent to Mount Moriah where his father planned to sacrifice him, but she wants to believe that through him the promise of life for all of God's people will be fulfilled. Mary will not see Jesus alive again after his ascent to Golgotha, but she knows that through his death and resurrection, the new covenant offers salvation to the world. So yes, if Sarah continues to illuminate believers with her splendor, Mary is indeed her worthy daughter.

The power of their "filiation" pushes us to continue our investigation into other biblical characters.

OTHER WOMEN, OFTEN PROPHETESSES

The first to catch our attention is Miriam, Moses's sister. This connection between Miriam and Mary starts with their names: Mary is only the English version of Miriam. Miriam of the First Testament, sister of Moses, is known for two reasons. The first is her ruse when she offers her mother's services to Pharaoh's daughter to take care of the baby Moses, abandoned on the Nile in a boat of straw and bitumen (Exod 2:1–10). Miriam therefore "drew Moses from the waters," as the etymology of his first name says. She is a figure of life winning over death. The second is her capacity for praise, when, just after the passage through the sea, on the shore of freedom, she takes up her tambourine and sings: "Sing to the Lord, for he has triumphed gloriously; horse and rider he has thrown into the sea" (Exod 15:21–22).Yet in a third instance (Num 12), Miriam distinguishes herself by her disobedience. Having criticized Moses for his marriage to a foreigner, she is struck with leprosy. Through Aaron's intercession, God commutes her fate to a seven-day exclusion from the camp.

Miriam is the first to have received the title of "virgin of Israel" of which we have spoken at length.[11] Two facts suggest this. The first is the constant infidelity to the Lord of the virgin of Israel, who makes a pact with idols. But, like Miriam, the virgin returns. This movement is repeated throughout Israel's history. Miriam, punished for her jealousy then forgiven, thus illustrates this ambivalence of the people. The second is the association, unique in the Bible, of the virgin of Israel with dancing. When Jeremiah says: "Again I will build you, and you shall be built, O virgin Israel! Again you shall take your tambourines, and go forth in the dance of the merrymakers" (Jer 31:4), he clearly refers to Miriam. Mary of the Gospels inherits this title and fulfills it; she is the virgin of Israel docile to the calls of the Spirit, even if they are transgressive. The kinship between Miriam and Mary is visible, and the evolution is too.

Let us now briefly discuss the prophetesses, beginning with Deborah, a figure linked to the origins of Israel, even before the institution of royalty. Her story is told in the oldest book of the Bible. Deborah was a "judge in Israel," a broader function than this term would suggest; she governed.[12] The Book of Judges presents her thus: "At that time Deborah, a prophetess, wife of Lappidoth,[13] was judging Israel....and the Israelites came up to her for judgement" (Judg 4:4–5). Her role will be decisive, because she appears during a time of troubles. At that time, the people, according to a formula that will become classic, "again did what was evil in the sight of the LORD" (Judg 4:1). Severely oppressed by the Canaanites, Israel returns to God and "cried out to the LORD" (Judg 4:3). Then comes providential help in the person of Deborah, who appoints Barak as war chief and who, until victory, indicates his mission to him in the face of powerful enemies. The contribution of Deborah, at once judge, prophetess, and political leader, is beginning to be recognized by commentators today, but very late.

Other female characters have earned the title of prophetess. The biblical scholar Irmtraud Fischer,[14] challenging preconceived ideas, mentions other women, including Huldah, a prophetess who will close the prophetic cycle of the Bible. What can we credit her with? Consulted by King Josiah in his fight against false gods and his promotion of the Book of Deuteronomy, a book that renews the law of Moses, Huldah, in the name of the Lord, reinforces Josiah in his choices. This proves that the supposed male exclusivity of the prophets attests to a very opportune laziness.

Later, Queen Esther will save and protect the Hebrew people and the faith in one God. A simple concubine who became queen in the harem of the Persian king Ahasuerus, through her beauty, her intelligence, and her sincerity she saved her people from the extermination plan hatched by the king's advisor. Let us salute her self-denial because, at the end of the story, she will retire and leave her uncle Mordecai in charge of affairs.[15]

Like Mary, women such as Esther and Judith contributed to the glory of God's people without ever being given any power of governance. The example of these prophetesses shows that it will be no surprise if, in our investigation, we call Mary the great prophetess. Many of the traits of one or the other of these women apply to Mary as well. In view of these relationships, we can attribute to Mary the titles of matriarch and prophetess.

Moreover, among these women of the First Testament, four appear in the genealogy of Jesus proposed by Matthew. We devote the following chapter to them.

6

FOUR SUBVERSIVE WOMEN

THE FOUR WOMEN we will now discuss prove the capacity for subversion, not only of Matthew who wrote the genealogy of Jesus in which they appear (see Matt 1:1–17) but of the Jewish expectation of a messiah, a movement that gave birth to Christianity. More directly, these women, who were briefly discussed in the previous chapter, will shed light on the figure of Mary. They are obviously not there by chance; they show how God's plan of salvation makes its way where it was probably not expected. This plan was to be embodied, according to the oracles of the prophets, in a messiah (*messiah* in Hebrew, *christos* in Greek), the one who, through anointing, receives the spirit of God in order to lead God's people. This messiah was to come from the lineage of the great King David.

From the first verse of his Gospel, Matthew therefore sets out to place Mary's son in this lineage: "Jesus, son of David, son of Abraham." He places Jesus among his people, the people God has chosen to reveal God to the nations. Many artists, illuminators, and master glassmakers have translated this message into images in splendid family trees that bear the name "Tree of Jesse," named after David's father. From the belly of the peacefully sleeping Jesse comes a tree whose upper branches shelter Mary and her child.

To help enter into the structure of this genealogy, a common genre in the Bible, it must be remembered that at the time of

Matthew, a woman never appeared in what is called the *toledôth*. Even if women ensured the continuity of families in their bodies, only men—fathers—were mentioned, according to precise rules (natural descent, legal descent), because more than blood, what mattered was the durability of the name, of the House, of the one who sponsored it.

Nevertheless, in the genealogy reported by Matthew—an author not inclined to transgression—four women are named before Mary. After the surprise of finding them in this family tree, let us identify what unites them. They all lived in transgressive, subversive situations. However, Matthew does not disapprove of them; through his frequent reading of the scriptures, he engages his own faith that the Spirit can influence the course of history by unexpected changes of direction that, sometimes, subvert common laws.

The first of these women is called Tamar. She is the daughter-in-law of Judah, one of the twelve sons of the patriarch Jacob. She will find a very curious way to give descendants to her in-laws (see Gen 38). Having become a widow, she must, according to the Jewish law called "levirate marriage,"[1] marry her brother-in-law Onan, but he tries to back out. He then perishes in return for having let his seed fall on the ground, rather than give it to his sister-in-law.

Widowed again, faced with the refusal of her father-in-law to give her his third and last son because he feared that he, too, would die, she veils her face, a sign of prostitution, and watches for the passage of her father-in-law. Judah, not knowing who she is, has sexual relations with her. Soon pregnant, she is discovered, and her father-in-law must come to her aid and accept the child. Judah, however, cunning, sometimes dishonest, draws an extraordinary conclusion from this adventure which, in a questionable way, nevertheless gave him descendants: "She is more in the right than I" (Gen 38:26).

The second woman mentioned by Matthew is Rahab, described in the Book of Joshua (chapter 2). Let us remember: The people are wandering in the desert and seeking to enter the Promised Land. Their leader, Joshua, is preparing to conquer the land "flowing with milk and honey," according to the Bible's formula, and he surrounds the city of Jericho with its famous walls. Two of his men sent on reconnaissance are hidden by a woman, Rahab. Thanks to her directions, the city is taken, and the woman's family is saved. But the Bible specifies that she is a prostitute, and what is more, a Canaanite, therefore both immoral and foreign.... These two pieces of information are not without spiciness concerning a woman who belongs to the genealogy given to Christ. However, the text shows that she is intelligent, cunning, and, above all, animated by faith in the God of Israel.

The third woman listed is related to Rahab since she will marry her son, Boaz. This is Ruth, a foreigner from the country of Moab, the ancestral enemy of Israel. Ruth does not distinguish herself by a transgression, but she shows exceptional compassion toward Naomi, her mother-in-law, a widow who has lost her sons and is therefore without resources. She follows her when she returns to her native land, Israel. Following the cunning advice of her mother-in-law, this young widow seduces the master of the field where she is allowed to glean, in a manner that is not without some spiciness:

> Now here is our kinsman Boaz, with whose young women you have been working. See, he is winnowing barley tonight at the threshing-floor. Now wash and anoint yourself, and put on your best clothes and go down to the threshing-floor; but do not make yourself known to the man until he has finished eating and drinking. When he lies down, observe the place where he lies; then, go and uncover his feet and lie down; and he will tell you what to do. (Ruth 3:2–4)

Ruth will, nevertheless, become the grandmother of King David, which explains her presence in this genealogy.

The fourth woman, finally, is Uriah's wife, Bathsheba, whom King David coveted for her great beauty (see 2 Sam 11). After he impregnates her, David summons Uriah and tries to cajole him to go down to his house, hoping he will have sex with his wife and thus the child will be assumed to be is, but Uriah, ever the faithful warrior, refuses—twice. It is then that David gives the order for Uriah to be placed in the front line of the battle so that he dies. Bathsheba, after having lost the child of adultery, becomes the mother of Solomon, who became king after his father David. The choice of this woman differs a little from the previous ones. It illustrates both the responsibility of women for the succession of generations and the chain of links that lead to reprehensible acts. It is not Bathsheba who sinned, but David's fault cannot but concern her, just as it concerns all his descendants.

Mary, cited in fifth place, is thus preceded by models who reveal something about the intervention of women in the course of the history of the Hebrew people. Each supports the revelation of Jesus, the Christ.

First of all, traditional moral laws are shaken up, as much for these four women as for Mary, pregnant without a husband.

Then the inclusion of two foreign women relativizes, even denounces, the withdrawal into the chosen people alone, and it invites us to the universalism advocated by Jesus on the cross.

Further, these four women prove that the barriers of social exclusion are inoperative in the eyes of God. Mary, like Tamar, Rahab, Ruth, or Bathsheba, does not care about the risk of social disapproval. God, who chooses them, also does not care. Their determination, based on their faith, unwaveringly transgresses the patriarchal rules to which they are expected to adhere.

Finally, the intervention of these women in critical moments when it is a question of saving the faith in the true God and transmitting it cannot be erased. At every critical moment in the history of this recalcitrant people, every time a crisis appears or an impasse seems to be coming, a woman rises up and opens the way by an unexpected act, sometimes not in accordance with the law of Moses. Today, we would call these acts "disruptive." Here again, Mary conforms with these examples; it is she who is the "cause" of salvation by her yes.

Finally, let us observe how these women know how to receive the Spirit who guides them in their faith and pushes them to accept improbable human choices. Tamar tries the impossible to give descendants to the tribe of Judah. Rahab, because she has known the power of the one God who is capable of bringing the Hebrew people out of the land of servitude, sides with Joshua against her own people. Why does Ruth, this young Moabite widow, decide to follow her Jewish mother-in-law Naomi who returns to the country where nothing and no one awaits her, where she will be badly received and promised poverty? As for Bathsheba, she insures that her son Solomon will indeed be the one to succeed David: "My lord, you swore to your servant by the LORD your God, saying: Your son Solomon shall succeed me as king" (1 Kings 1:17). David has him anointed with the help of the prophet Nathan: "Have my son Solomon ride on my own mule, and bring him down to Gihon. There let the priest Zadok and the prophet Nathan anoint him king over Israel" (1 Kings 1:33–34).

Certainly, all these women are compassionate, but they are guided by an unwavering faith in the power of the Spirit of God, a God who is not always theirs originally. Between these free, daring women and Mary, the parallel gradually emerges. Mary confirms and amplifies the choices of those who preceded her in a transgression whose scope we never cease to recall. Much more than the obedience that is so vaunted by tradition, the capacity to bear shame, mockery, and danger must be emphasized. We can see behind this lesson the concept of a personal conscience before its time, which brings into harmony the conscience and faith of a person without worrying about the image she will project.

7

MARY, AN IMAGE OF ISRAEL

THIS CHAPTER WILL familiarize us with a common practice of biblical authors, that of making characters bear the burden of embodying a "figure." Mary, we will show, is placed by Luke in the story of the annunciation (see Luke 1:26–38) as the figure of all Israel. Let us first identify what is contained in this term that we have used several times without really explaining it. The writers of scripture do not keep a factual chronicle, they do not draw portraits in the manner of a modern novelist, but they are concerned with "edifying" the audience, "building them up" in order to guide them in their relationships with God. For this, they speak "in figures." Practically all the biblical characters, from Abraham and Sarah up to the Samaritan woman, if they appear as historical heroes, have above all an incontestable capacity to be symbolic supports that speak to faith.

A figure is an "emblematic person," the archetype of a human attitude, which can illustrate a tribe or a people. It has a dimension of initiation, support, and reference. The prophets made great use of figures, and so did the authors of the New Testament, for example with Judas.[1] By reading the story of the annunciation, we will discover that its very structure leads us to "see" the people of Israel as a whole behind the "figure" of Mary, this young girl with the most common first name in Israel, who lives in a town so little known to authors of the time that it illustrates them all.

To justify our point, let us underline a detail that is very often ignored, but which, once spotted, radically changes the way we can look at this story: It has no witnesses. Just perhaps a frightened cat as in the annunciation painted by Lorenzo Lotto....[2] We are in front of an intimate scene. But then, who tells us about it? Would we have benefited from confidences from Mary? Would she have spoken to Joseph, who would have told it to Luke? Or did Luke construct his story? But if Luke constructed it "from scratch," we would still need to know which parts.

To support this disconcerting observation, let us see if there is at least one contemporary of Mary who could have contributed, through their memories, to establishing the chronicle of her life. Around the year 70, at the time when Luke finished his Gospel, writing the two chapters called the "infancy narratives," Mary would have been between eighty-five and ninety-five years old. No one can exclude the possibility that she reached this great age, nor that she reported the facts to her relatives, perhaps, many years before Luke took up his pen. If this were the case, Luke, whose concern for reliable information is well known (see Luke 1:3), could have mentioned his sources, or even, for a story of such supreme importance, inserted into his text the witness of this story, by the process of *storytelling* that is widely used today but is as old as writing. If he did not do so, if he took the risk of delivering to his readers a story without witnesses, could it not be because that is his underlying intention?

AN ANNOUNCEMENT TO THE READER

This is the path we will take now, in order to explore all its riches. If this story is deliberately without witnesses, we must admit that it was constructed by Luke. For the reader, this is a considerable, even dizzying piece of news. How can we know what really happened in the house of young Mary? The reader is thus obliged to seek out the heart of the message, to find the revelation hidden within it. Of course, along the way, the reader will question the trust placed in the writer. Is Luke credible? If the reader believes him, this story is internalized, and the reader becomes an essential actor in the process, not only of its reception but also of the transmission of the story. This questioning suggests that beyond the "announcement made to Mary," there is an "announcement made to the reader," who is called upon to make a decision. We have just defined the setting of this announcement: It is a story without witnesses. It remains to retrace its path and discover the heart of the message being delivered.

First, let us ask ourselves how Luke goes about it. What attitudes does he attribute to Mary? He makes this story the initial scene in which the young girl who will be at the heart of the plan of salvation appears. Luke must therefore capture his audience with scenes that are familiar to them. Now, there are biblical themes well known to all of Israel that resonate in the mind of every Jewish reader. Thus, Mary receives the *visit* of the angel in the same way that God visits God's people. She is *filled with grace*, that is, *chosen* by the Lord as the people were, by pure divine mercy.[3] Mary does not refuse to hear the angel; she *listens*. She *fears* God, as does Israel, a notion that is easily understood if we keep in mind the verse pronounced by Moses at the entry of the Hebrew people into the Promised Land: "The Lord your God you shall follow, him alone you shall fear, his commandments you shall keep, his voice you shall obey, him you shall serve, and to him you shall hold fast" (Deut 13:4). The fear of God, in the Bible, has a positive sense; it is not terror but that respectful attachment, an engagement with the good, of the one who follows his God. Mary exhibits the desire for a God who, even if the relationship is asymmetrical, is her unwavering ally.

Then, by the question that Mary asks—"How can this be since I am a virgin?"—the young girl shows at the same time that she wants to understand, that she is available to the Spirit, and that she is *searching*, a central principle of Jewish spirituality. The search, or *derech*, is a disposition of mind, an attitude before the world, an awakened desire, an appetite, and even a greediness for life, the work of the Creator. To be constantly in search of God is the first instruction that Judaism gives to its members. Mary possesses this quality offered to all the people.

Finally, Mary makes *a covenant*, according to the great model of the covenant proposed in the Book of Exodus (see Exod 24) and the Book of Joshua (see Josh 24), where all Israel chooses the Lord. Like Israel, Mary says yes; she obeys God, that is, she listens and accepts the divine proposal. At the risk of transgressing the moral order of the patriarchy, she adheres to God's plan.

Therefore, this story of Luke resumes the great biblical themes that construct the relationship of the believer to God: visitation, election, and covenant. The three responses of Mary are the qualities requested of Israel—fear, searching, and that which precedes them and provides their foundation—listening, according to the central prayer to the one God, which begins, "Hear O Israel" (Deut 6:4). Through all these analogies, Luke allows his reader to discover that this young girl, in perpetual search, ready to find in all things the presence and action of God, is a "figure" for all of Israel who welcomes the child and fulfills the promise of a savior messiah. Thus Luke, who perhaps never saw Mary, painted the young Jewish girl according to the heart of God. As this evocative title says, he paints the *Portrait of Israel as a Young Girl.*[4] She is "the Israel of God" who, like her, preserved herself from idols; she is the "virgin of Israel" already mentioned.[5]

In addition to these qualities required of Israel, there are the characteristics that Luke wants to give to Mary in the episode of the annunciation, as Luca Castiglioni explains: "The way in which Mary accepts the angel's proposal highlights her inner freedom, her capacity for self-determination and her conscious and active faith....She decides on her life without letting social and religious interference hinder her availability."[6] The major consequence of this metaphorical use of a character raised to the rank of a figure is to shatter any claim to make Mary a model for women alone.

We have already observed that Jewish prophecy symbolizes the union of God with God's people using the image of the wedding. God is in a masculine position, the people—men and women—in a feminine position. We are in a poetic register, neither anthropological nor legal. It is therefore not surprising for the readers of Luke that the men of Israel find themselves in a symbolic role that is the opposite of their gender. Nor is it surprising that women understand and admit that it is not their femininity that is at stake, but their collective identity before God. It is a pity that the Latin spirit inherited by Roman Catholicism with its juristic impulses has crushed this richness.

In conclusion, let us remember that Luke, in this "inaugural" story, sets out his entire project through Mary, the figure of Israel. A savior is promised to us. If this young girl welcomed him, as a prefiguration of all Israel, any reader can do the same.

ANNA AND SIMEON, GODPARENTS OF THE CHILD

Once we acknowledge that Mary represents all of Israel and that this figure is not gendered, we must again acknowledge that Mary is not the center of this project. We will be even more convinced of this by looking more closely at the two chapters that Luke devotes to the childhood of Jesus. On the one hand, Mary will prepare for the reception of her son in his social environment; how will he be accepted in Israel and beyond, and by whom? On the other hand, this project will also be carried out by other stakeholders: Elizabeth, the angel Gabriel, John the Baptist, Joseph, the shepherds, Simeon and Anna.

Previously, Luke put another actor on stage, charged with showing the failure of the temple officials. This is Zechariah, a priest, a just and irreproachable man, but who doubts the word of the angel who came to announce to him the late pregnancy of his wife Elizabeth. Because of this, this priest who is supposed to announce the coming of the savior will lose his essential attribute: the word (see Luke 1:5–25).[7] Zechariah's silence illustrates a temple that has become mute.

In contrast, at the end of these two chapters, Simeon and Anna will be the real interlocutors of the temple. Mary and Joseph will meet them when, like all parents of a newborn, they go there to "present him to the Lord" (Luke 2:22). There, Simeon and Anna will receive them in place of the missing officials. This double recognition, by a man and a woman, already has a slightly subversive flavor compared to the clerical personnel. Anna, named "prophetess," will illustrate the prophetic function, essential because it announces salvation that the temple should express but that, like most overly established institutions, it almost always rejects. With authority, but also an unusual and undisguised tenderness, Simeon the wise, a figure of the past, of the scriptures whose guarantee it is important to obtain—and the only man of the Gospels to take Jesus in his arms—will express his gratitude for having seen with his eyes the "salvation...of all peoples," "light...to the Gentiles," and the "glory to your people Israel" (Luke 2:29–32).

But he will also darken the parents' joy by announcing to Mary that "a sword will pierce your own soul" (Luke 2:35). He acknowledges, very early in the life of this child and in the heart of his mother, that salvation will come through the cross. In this, Simeon plays the role of a godfather to the child's parents, a figure on whom they can rely, in the way that a believer relies on the scriptures. He certifies that this child is indeed the one Israel was waiting for, saying, "my eyes have seen your salvation" (Luke 2:30), and he names a painful future.

Anna's function is different; she is the communicator of the duo, and in an implicit complicity with the young mother, she seems naturally to take over. In two verses of extreme density, Luke shows how much Anna continues Mary's work of childbirth (see Luke 2:36–38).

In the biblical account, this old woman succeeds Huldah, the last of the prophetesses cited by the scriptures (see 2 Kings 22:8–20), as we have shown.[8] Just as Huldah had supported the discovery of the "Book of the Covenant" found in the temple,[9] so too, Anna supports the Gospel—the good news—that Luke is going to offer to the Jewish people; it is the new "Book of the Covenant." Luke places Anna both on the threshold of his book and in the place from which, according to him, salvation must come, the temple. Indeed, Luke insists on this since he gives her the last sentence of his book: "They were continually in the temple blessing God" (Luke 24:53).

But to make pronouncements in place of the official authorities, Anna needs a legitimacy that she is far from possessing. By what right could she speak in their name? Well, just as Judith and

Esther subverted the codes in force in their societies, so Anna will gain, in the eyes of Luke and his audience, an authority that was completely improbable. Besides being a woman, which puts her more on the side of the "voiceless," Anna has another handicap. She does not come from Jerusalem, the place of priestly aristocracy and arrogance. She comes from the tribe of Asher, far to the north, the most remote, the most insignificant, the muddiest land in Israel. But she has two assets that Luke will claim count for more than official titles.

The first is her age! She is eighty-four, a multiple of both seven, the number of completion, and of twelve, that of the tribes of Israel. This number gives Anna the authority necessary to announce to all Israel that the times are "fulfilled." Above all, Luke reports that she has moral power; she lives in the temple serving God "with fasting and prayer night and day" (2:37). This allows third parties to welcome both her femininity and the insignificance of her tribe; she has no function, but her life is in the service of God. Thus, from two sources of respect, and associated with two other improbable qualities, which God does not disdain but sometimes even privileges—her femininity and modesty—Anna rises legitimately to the rank of speaker in place of the absent officials. What a reversal! Indeed, if she becomes able to officially represent the temple, her word acquires considerable value. As Judith had done before her, she can speak in the name of all Israel and to all Israel.

But she is not going to be satisfied with that. Her new legitimacy is not for her, but for the child, as Luke specifies. Anna begins "to speak about the child to all who were looking for the redemption of Jerusalem" (2:38). Luke shows that this child is indeed the one that the scriptures announced and that the people were waiting for. By offering this newborn the power of her word, Anna, as a busy and devoted older sister, continues Mary's work of childbirth. She introduces the child into public religious life and legitimizes his messianic character. One could say that she sets herself up as godmother to the child, of whom Simeon would be the godfather.

BEYOND THE STORY

At the end of these two chapters, the "announcement to the reader" is not yet complete. The heart of the message still awaits—to invite readers to consider themselves as members of the Israel of God, docile to the voice of the Lord. Israel is not a speaker from the past but is contemporary with the reader. Christians read the scriptures knowing that the word of the Lord to Israel is also addressed to them. The story thus moves into the very existence of the one who receives it. If by chance an angel, that is to say a "messenger of God" whose form is not defined, bursts into one's home, under the cover of an encounter, a reading, a prayer, and "speaks," leading the person toward a cause, a service—perhaps transgressive—in which one sees the hand of the Lord, all one has left to do is discern, as Mary did, and to consider this yes that can change one's life. Luke goes that far. His story is a powerful exhortation to the reader.

Luke, however, was speaking to Jews who decoded the double or triple meanings of his story more spontaneously than a modern reader, whose confusion is understandable. If Mary is a figure "constructed" according to the broad outlines of Jewish spirituality, we are entitled to ask ourselves whether the "real Mary" existed. Does she remain a person "of history"? The answer is obvious: If Jesus existed, he had a mother. Let us remember the legal adage: *Sola mater certa est* (only the mother is certain). How Mary behaved in history, we will never know exactly, and it is not important. Beyond contemporary fixations on the question of historical veracity, it is the "figure" of Mary that counts; it is she who teaches. Mary, the figure of Israel, looks toward the son, the savior. This is what the construction of Luke attests to; after this annunciation, and the visitation that follows it, he will have Mary pronounce her masterpiece, the Magnificat. We will verify that it is already the life program of the son.

8

THE MAGNIFICAT

IN OUR PROJECT to restore to the figure of Mary the vigor of her original colors, the Magnificat (Luke 1:46–55) is, with the story of the annunciation, one of the key pieces. Certainly, it comes quite easily to everyone's lips, sometimes for the beauty of the song or for the explosion of praise that it carries within it, but if we analyze it closely, all the audacity of Mary bursts forth and reveals, before her son, the "evangelical radicalness" which, because it characterizes the son, becomes that of the mother. The tone that Mary uses anticipates that of Jesus in the Beatitudes and the Sermon on the Mount, which are the key programmatic discourses. Faced with the vigor of her words, one thing comes to mind: What other declaration more than this one better expresses the good news, her own contribution to the ministry of her Son, and the new covenant that he brings?

Let us first recall that Luke, through the numerous allusions that celebrate the God of the covenant "in favor of Abraham and his descendants forever," further underlines that Mary is the daughter of Abraham, heiress of Sarah, anchored in faith in the one God.

This additional formal link between the two testaments explains why, in the background of the Magnificat, the canticle of Hannah (1 Sam 2), the mother of the prophet Samuel, bursts forth. The parallel is not just a simple allusion. Let us return for a moment to the tragedy that Hannah experienced. The young woman was sterile, and "she was deeply distressed and prayed to the LORD, and wept bitterly" (1 Sam 1:10) for God to give her a son. The priest Eli, seeing her crying while praying, thinks she is drunk, so much does her voice waver in her supplication. Samuel is born from this answered prayer. Then Hannah sings a song of praise and joy.

WHEN GOD'S PURPOSE IS FULFILLED

When Hannah concludes her song with, "He will give strength to his king, and exalt the power of his anointed" (1 Sam 2:10), she announces the coming of the Messiah, the one who has received the anointing with oil. Although Luke does not put this passage into the mouth of Mary, a Jewish reader knows very well that a partial quotation of a text also evokes the rest of it, even if unsaid. And since the "melody" of Hannah's song is a classic for the Jewish reader, the reader cannot help but be struck by the proximity of intention between the two texts.

AN ELOQUENT COMPARISON

In addition to containing many other biblical references, Mary's song is strongly inspired by that of Hannah. The parallels below (in italics) underlines, by the extent of the borrowings, the deep rooting of the Magnificat in the scriptures.

Canticle of Hannah 1 Samuel 2:1–10	*Canticle of Mary* Luke 1:46–55
[1] Hannah prayed and said: "*My heart exults in the* L*ORD*; my strength is exalted in my God. My mouth derides my enemies, because *I rejoice in my victory.*	[46] And Mary said: "*My soul magnifies the Lord,* [47]and *my spirit rejoices in God / my Savior,* [48] for he has looked with favor on the lowliness of his servant. Surely, from now on *all generations* will call me blessed;
[2] *There is no Holy One like the* L*ORD*, no one besides you; there is no rock like our God.	[49] for the Mighty One has done great things for me, and *holy is his name.*

[3] Talk no more so very proudly, let not arrogance come from your mouth; for the LORD is a God of knowledge and by him actions are weighed.	[50] His mercy is for those who fear him from generation to generation
[4] The *bows of the mighty are broken,* but the feeble gird on strength.	[51] *He has shown strength with his arm;* he has scattered the proud in the thoughts of their hearts.
[5] Those who were full have hired themselves out for bread, but those who were hungry are fat with spoil The barren has borne seven, but she who has many children is forlorn.	
[6] The LORD kills and brings to life; he brings down to Sheol and raises up.	
[7] The *LORD makes poor and makes rich;* *he brings low, he also exalts.*	[52] *He has brought down the powerful from their thrones,* *and lifted up the lowly;*
[8] *He raises up the poor from the dust;* *he lifts the needy from the ash heap,* *to make them sit with princes* *and inherit a seat of honor.* For the pillars of the earth are the LORD's and on them he has set the world.	[53] *he has filled the hungry with good things,* *and sent the rich away empty.*
[9] He will guard the feet of his faithful ones, but the wicked shall be cut off in darkness; for not by might does one prevail. [10] The LORD! His adversaries shall be shattered; / the Most High will thunder in heaven. / The LORD will judge the ends of the earth; / he will give strength to his king, / *and exalt the power of his anointed."*	[54] He has helped his servant Israel, in remembrance of his mercy, [55] according to the promise he made to our ancestors, *to Abraham and to his descendants for ever."*

All these references to scripture remind us how much Mary adopts them and is their spokesperson. As the mother of the Messiah, she participates in the fulfillment of the Word. The reader of Luke is invited to realize this. If Mary, as soon as she speaks, says: "My soul magnifies the Lord and my spirit rejoices in God my Savior," let us not see in this the euphoria of a young woman awaiting the birth of a child. She is not Elizabeth; Mary hoped for nothing, especially when she was young and not yet married. Moreover, she does not speak at all of her pregnancy or of the joy that it could bring her. If she exults with joy, we will see, verse after verse, that she perceives the fulfillment in her of God's plan announced by the prophecy of Isaiah: "Look, the young woman is with child" (Isa 7:14).

The central subject of her speech, the one whose omnipotence, greatness, holiness, and mercy she praises, and to whom she expresses all her gratitude for the benefits she has received from him, is her Lord. She cannot separate herself from God's presence. In the same invocation, this God is her *Savior*. Here again, Mary confesses a very lively faith, accompanied by the "fear of God." As we see, the whole song confesses a strong union between Mary and her Lord.

Finally, this song highlights that God's logic is not human logic. In God's eyes, the power of the great of this world confers no favor. Only God can do what is impossible for human beings, as Mary confessed in response to the angel's announcement. In what Mary experiences, which is perceived in her words, the reader detects the end to which her faith and commitment lead her. Here again, Mary who sings her joy at welcoming a savior does not come to tell a simple story of birth. We are not in a pattern of classical maternal bonds. This is why none of the four Gospels will mention any emotional ties between Jesus and his mother. On the contrary, Jesus will never cease to deconstruct family ties in favor of those of faith.

In fact, the Magnificat has a particular power. Mary already reveals what Christ will do. In the name of her son, as if she were assuming a sort of regency, but even more as a prophetess, Mary announces the program that will be confirmed by the discourse, known as the Beatitudes, that Jesus will give on the mountain before his disciples.

Let us examine more closely what she says. First, she affirms that the adventure she sets forth concerns the whole of time: "His mercy is for those who fear him from generation to generation" (Luke 1:50). The mercy in question refers to the salvation that is approaching since the Messiah is coming. Mary is joyful because scripture is fulfilled. We have already highlighted how Mary in the story of the annunciation integrates the whole history of Israel to lead it toward the kingdom, in an openness to the universal. Here, the expression "from generation to generation" confirms it, as does the last verse: "according to the promise he made to our ancestors, to Abraham and to his descendants for ever" (Luke 1:55). The universalization in time follows the announcement of that in space.

But the essential remains to be said. Through this song, Mary truly becomes the symbol of the elevation of the humble. Behind Mary's words, we have said that we must see Jesus's program. It is this Jesus-Messiah who is subversive, because he comes to overthrow the powerful from their thrones. Mary indicates this by denouncing all forms of humiliation ("he lifts up the lowly"), including slavery. This very human humiliation is more than abasement; it points to both devaluation and suffering. Humiliation at the time of Mary was that of a people reduced to bowing their backs under Roman domination, as they had too often been forced to bow to other imperial powers in the past. Mary's submission combines that of her people and that of all dominated human beings, whether because of their sex, their skin color, or their social condition. Let us remember that Mary is a woman in a patriarchal universe who could have been stoned for her illegitimate pregnancy and whose testimony is legally accepted by no one.

Furthermore, it is important to take into account the conjugation of verbs in the proclamation. All the verbs of which Jesus is the subject are in the past tense. The times are fulfilled. Mary's faith tells us that in Christ, liberation has already taken place. It remains to be implemented, both through personal spiritual work and through a commitment to serving our brothers and sisters in the world "already there."

What a reversal of the ideas we have received about the submission of Mary and the obedience to which she is supposed to invite us!

WHAT DO PEOPLE SAY ABOUT THE MAGNIFICAT TODAY?

Among the many comments of Popes John Paul II and Benedict XVI on the Magnificat, let us recall this one in which John Paul II links the Magnificat to the fate of women:

> Mary is the new beginning of the dignity and vocation of woman....The key to understanding this can be found in particular in the words placed by the Evangelist on Mary's lips after the Annunciation, during her visit to Elizabeth: "He has done great things for me" (Luke 1:49). These words obviously concern the conception of her Son, who is the Son of the Most High [see Luke 1:32], the Holy One of God, but at the same time, they can also mean the discovery of the feminine character of her humanity. The Almighty has done great things for me: such is the discovery of all the riches, of all the personal resources of femininity, of the eternal originality of the "woman" as God wanted her, a person in herself, who finds herself at the same time by the "disinterested gift of herself." (MD 11)

These interpretations are perplexing. Above all, the pope is seeking here to justify his own patriarchal system that defines a particular feminine vocation. We have amply emphasized that, under the guise of valuing women, the pope directs them toward being a wife and mother and makes Mary an idealized model of the feminine. If we think we have convinced our readers, in the preceding pages, that according to the scriptures, Mary is not a model reserved for women, we are even more certain that, according to the Magnificat, she is even less so! On what basis, for example, can the pope interpret the words: "the Mighty One has done great things for me" as "the discovery of the resources of femininity"? Also, what is the reference to the "disinterested gift of herself" doing in this text? John Paul II has an almost obstinate will to impose on every woman qualities that nothing allows us to attribute to Mary without a distortion the scriptures. Moreover, did the pope realize that he was thus depriving men of the power to appropriate a song that is essential to the faith? As for us, we do not believe that the point of this expression "great things" is exceptional motherhood, but rather the gift of faith that allowed Mary to answer "yes" to the angel. Once again, let us emphasize that it is not the modus operandi that matters in what happens to Mary, but the greatness of the God who made it possible.

Our perplexity is redoubled when we see the meager theological harvest proposed by Pope John Paul II. How far we are from a true analysis of the text, whether literary or theological! Why does John Paul II choose not to give anything "nourishing" to the women to whom he writes? Should we only speak to women about their femininity? This recalls these old practices where, in France there existed, among other discriminatory courses, a school of Higher Commercial Studies for boys and a "feminine polytechnic" school for young girls,[1] as if the rules of commerce and science were not the same for everyone. Civil society has evolved; the Church has not.

In the continuation of his argument, the pope identifies Mary with the Church, but here again he will, this time, decline its instrumentalization starting from the Eucharist. The goal? To exalt the greatness of priests, and to this end, subordinate women to men:

> In the Eucharist, the redemptive act of Christ the Bridegroom towards the Church, the Bride is expressed above all sacramentally. This becomes transparent and unequivocal when the sacramental service of the Eucharist, where the priest acts *in persona Christi*, is carried out by man. (MD 22)

It is verified once again, in this statement, how much the weakening of the clerical body pushes the magisterium to a worrying "war of the genders." In general, the institution, when it explains what these "great things" are, praises the motherhood of Mary and underlines in the Magnificat the power of faith in mercy, rather than deepening the analysis. Because then it would have to drastically modify its practices, especially with regard to all the discriminated people of the earth, the exploited, the excluded.

THE CONTRIBUTION OF LIBERATION THEOLOGIANS

Liberation theologians were not mistaken in seeing, from the first word of the Magnificat, a subversive basis available for the recognition of the oppressed all over the world but particularly in Latin America where, in the 1970s to 1980s, they developed this theological current.

The Peruvian Dominican Gustavo Gutiérrez (1928–2024) is considered the father of this movement, named after his book *Theology of Liberation*, published in 1973. This theology, which emerged in countries of dictatorships with very unequal development, offers an essential response to the oppressed. According to its author, it tells the poor that their current situation is not wanted by God and that they are, for the Gospel, the "neighbor" par excellence.

This theology finds its model in Moses's liberation of the Hebrews oppressed in Egypt, but it also pays particular attention to the figure of Mary, who is considered by these theologians "as a woman of the people, close to the poor and the excluded,"[2] according to the words of Dominique Cerbelaud. "Filled with grace," a gift from God, Mary announces her liberation to humanity, which is victimized by oppressions of all kinds—political, societal, and so many others. Under their new gaze, another face of Mary succeeds in being constructed. Faced with a mythical Queen of Heaven and an eternal Virgin, feminist theology, driven by that of liberation, finds in Mary a figure of a woman who cannot be read in terms of submission-domination, but who is free and capable of making her own decisions when, for example, it is a question of virginity.

It is this "progressive" reading of the Magnificat that Gustavo Gutiérrez espouses by presenting it as "one of the texts of the New Testament whose political and liberating content is the most intense." Indeed, what exploited population, reading: "He has brought down the powerful from their thrones, and lifted up the lowly; he has filled the hungry with good things, and sent the rich away empty," would not be challenged? In this context, the Magnificat is read as a program of social justice to be implemented as an anticipated realization of the kingdom such as one finds in the First Testament, in particular in the defeat of pharaoh, justifying the struggles for liberation.

The humble and the poor are not always so only because of a lack of economic resources. They can be victims of dehumanization of all kinds, bending under the yoke of dictatorships that reduce them to slavery or to flight. Thus, Jürgen Moltmann calls for joining them in their misery by inviting "solidarity with those who are at the bottom of the social ladder and who are humiliated."[3] He also quotes Gustavo Gutiérrez from *Theology of Liberation*, who specifies that "Christian poverty, an expression of love, is in solidarity with the poor and a protest against poverty."[4] Finally, Leonardo Boff also rooted his commitment to the poor of Latin America in Mary, as seen in the Magnificat.

Faced with these vigorous affirmations that take Mary and particularly the Magnificat as their standard, the Catholic institution, through the voice of John Paul II, was very critical. In 1984, an "instruction," *Libertatis Nuntius*, established by the Congregation for the Doctrine of the Faith (directed by Cardinal Joseph Ratzinger), judged the interest in the poor to be praiseworthy, but nevertheless concluded that liberation theology is incompatible with the doctrine of the faith. Furthermore, he quickly returned to this excessive condemnation, but added a second note, in March 1986, that reluctantly welcomed the spiritual dimension of this theology of freedom.

Justice was done when Pope Francis received Father Gustavo Gutiérrez.[5] Francis, through his welcome and openness to the poor and migrants, thus joined Jürgen Moltmann: "For a Christian, there is no alternative between evangelization and humanization. There is no alternative between interior conversion and change in relationships and living conditions,...there is no alternative between the humanity and the divinity of Jesus."[6] In short, a Christian must be able to make a change in his interior landscape at the same time as a change in the living conditions of the world around him.

This is why Moltmann explains that if the title "Christ" means redeemer and liberator, a Christian praxis can only aim at the liberation of the human being from his inhumanity. Both sides are essential, and Pope Francis clearly recalled the need to return both to the word of God, to discover and love ever more the person of Jesus Christ, and to pay attention to the poorest, to implement the commandments of love.

Certainly, these foundational remarks need to be confronted with the reality and complexity of political situations. We have seen that the verbs of the Magnificat are formulated in the past tense. This song announces a liberation that has already taken place and that must extend "from generation to generation." However, if it is the "general political discourse of the Mother of God," if it is the prefiguration of what her son will experience during the three years of his public ministry and during the passion, it says nothing about the practical modalities of current support for the poor. They are to be invented according to the contexts, but without erasing the radical nature of the message. The Magnificat must put its readers to work! In any case, it is a powerful encouragement to a united and reconciled humanity.

This song, thus placed, is the high point of Mary's response to the manifestation she received from God. This song of praise that communicates her being is entirely woven from her ardent faith. We discover a woman full of courage, lucidity, and incredible dynamism. Mary is not the bland being confined in foolish submission that we have been offered for centuries but a precious companion for those who believe, which, far from altering the veneration that we can have for her, can, on the contrary, only exalt her.

MARY'S LARGE CLOAK

Although the figure of Mary has encountered some resistance from feminist movements and Christian intellectuals, she is not without defenders on the theological level. A new closer look at the text stimulates reflection, as demonstrated by the Uruguayan theologian Maria Teresa Porcile Santiso.[7]

Porcile Santiso is interested in Mary[8] for what she calls her "inner space," and reconstructs the figure of Mary from the Magnificat as the bodily space of the "inhabited Church." To make these somewhat hermetic formulas more accessible, let us think of the classic image of the large blue cloak worn by Mary, wide open and crowded inside with the small silhouettes of the faithful. The believers whom Mary shelters are those who form the Church of her son.

Before the angel leaves her, when Mary says "let it be with me according to your word" (Luke 1:38), she offers her own body to the new Creation. By receiving the Spirit, she becomes "God's dwelling place," full of hope. She, who has sheltered the Son of God in her body, actualizes this indwelling in the life of faith of believers and therefore of the Church.

This reality of faith suggests to this theologian that Mary is called as a disciple to various ministries. Mary assumes the ministry of spirituality that is the "indwelling of the Spirit." This way of welcoming the Spirit into oneself, this spiritual "incorporation" of which Mary is the model from chapters 1 and 2 of Luke, can inspire every believer. Indeed, how in a meditation of faith can we exhaust the mystery of this yes to the Spirit? Mary is the teacher of us all. Even more: In Mary will be found the "ministry of the community," which manifests itself at Cana, at the foot of the cross, and at Pentecost. With this unusual title, but whose content is familiar, the theologian shows how Mary, through two other yeses that the text implies, accepts the responsibility that Christ on the cross gives her, to build the community shared with the beloved disciple and then with the Twelve on the morning of Pentecost. In her collaboration with the incarnation of the Word of God, she also contributes to revealing the trinitarian mystery. The Magnificat bears witness to this since "in God" she gives flesh to the son she received from the Spirit. She attests just as much to her prophetic ministry by announcing a merciful God who cares for the weak and elevates them by becoming like them.

In this way, Mary embodies in a privileged way "Mother of the Church," and as Maria Teresa Porcile Santiso says, "she is its most perfect figure." "Perfect" obviously does not mean actual. But Mary is the reference that the Church gives itself to become perfect. Here we verify how much Luke's proposition is confirmed and extended, seeing in Mary the figure of an Israel perfectly docile to God's call.

Thanks to this patient and sometimes demanding investigative work, we are now in possession of our major pieces of evidence. We are far from the disembodied and pale figure of a sweet and purring piety that is too often served to us!

Throughout the pages of this second part, we have discovered the major role of Mary in the history of salvation, precisely because she remains "ordered" to the glory of her Son. First, we highlighted the contribution of several women in the Bible. All of them enrich the features of the figure of Mary. Then, we noted that Luke, in the story without witnesses of the annunciation, had drawn the portrait of Mary as a "perfect believer" according to the heart of God, as God asked of Israel when it entered the promised land. In short, Mary is the elder on whom every believer can build their faith. By rereading the Magnificat closely, we have shown that Mary's joy is born from the coming of salvation into the world, in the person of the Son of God. Finally, we have emphasized that Mary becomes, in this song, the spokesperson for the humble and the oppressed, announcing the program of Jesus.

Now we can reconstruct the figure of Mary as the Gospels present it to us.

Part 3
RECONSTRUCTION

FROM CHAPTER TO CHAPTER, our investigation advances toward its end. Now we need to piece together what is still scattered into a more clearly defined outline. In the next four chapters, we will simply relate why and how Mary is the "excellent student" of the Gospels. First, we will show how the latter reaffirms her total humanity. Then in two more theological chapters, we will try to understand how she is, at the same time, mother of Jesus and mother of Christ. This will finally lead us to note that the deep intention of the authors of the New Testament is to present her as the accomplished model of the disciple. Let us not believe, however, that the "prize of excellence" that we award her suggests a wise, deserving, and docile child to the masters. It is rather the opposite! Mary, "filled with grace" according to the words of the angel Gabriel, radical in her choices, figure of an Israel that welcomes God, thwarts received ideas. She gives the example of a strong, free woman, feminist before her time, ultimately very modern. This discovery seemed so essential to us that we were surprised to think of how many commentators of the story had, intentionally, pushed Mary under the bushel basket, so dangerous did her freedom seem. But isn't it the same for Jesus?

9

MARY, NEVER TOO HUMAN

After having surveyed the scriptures, let us try, in this chapter, to approach this "Mary as you have never seen her before." One attribute that we suggest is that she is "never too human." The popular tropism that consists of extracting Mary's humanity from her is so strong that we must remember to protect ourselves from it. Human, yes, Mary is fully so, provided that we give all its depth to the expression "human." For Israel, humanity does not consist only in giving free rein to feelings, but in being responsible for oneself and for others. Thus, we underlined in the previous chapter that Mary's happiness was not "only" to be pregnant, but also to know that with this child-God, salvation had come near. According to Israel, and according to us, Sylvaine and Anne, humanity only truly exists if it includes, in its very definition, the quest for an afterlife, precisely the one announced by the Savior. Through his life, his healings, his teaching, and his passion, Christ shows the way toward a fulfilled, reconciled humanity, which leaves no one on its margins and knows itself to be called by someone greater than itself. Mary's humanity integrates this call. It is undoubtedly because this young woman has, in the strongest sense of the term, "lent herself to the plan of salvation" that she assumes the most eminent title granted to a human being among the people of Israel: She is a prophetess. Better than anyone else, she defends the cause of God, which is the task assigned to prophets, because she is the person closest to Jesus, who is both a man inserted into a precise moment in human history, and the Word of God, in other words Christ, one of the Trinity. Through this proximity, Mary also becomes the privileged companion of the believer who wants to meditate on the mystery of Christ. The initial and insurmountable place of the incarnation is the body of a woman.

MARY THE PROPHETESS

It is quite unusual to hear Mary referred to as a "prophetess." In common opinion, she is first and foremost a mother. And the Catholic Church so rarely speaks of prophetesses....Yet, even if the title is never awarded to her, it is hers, because Mary has the usual characteristics of prophets. Already, at the annunciation, the Holy Spirit came upon her (Luke 1:35), as it had formerly "fallen" upon the judges, upon the prophets, as well as upon King David.[1] It is a way of saying that the Spirit occupies them totally and assigns them what they must do. Mary, who knows the scriptures, understands that she is following in these footsteps. She knows that the judges were not magistrates in the modern sense of the word, but political leaders who ruled Israel before the country gave itself a king. The time of the judges is a more or less mythical period but one on which Israel projected the ideal of its relationship with God. At that time, there was no king and, according to the prophet Samuel, it was much better that way. The Bible says that then, at least in this matter, "the people followed the Lord." Mary is invited to do the same. She knows that prophecy is not the prerogative of exceptional people. It is offered to all, as the prophet Joel declares, "your sons and your daughters shall prophesy" (Joel 2:28). All this context prepares Mary for a serene acceptance of her prophetic identity. She also knows the mission of these chosen ones very well: They are neither soothsayers nor, strictly speaking, visionaries, but first and foremost "spokespeople" of the Lord. In time, and often out of time, they announce to the people their salvation, their deliverance, or the wrath of God. Precisely, in the time of Mary, there was lament; the prophets have fallen silent. Did they no longer have a place in Israel? Since the announcement to the prophet Daniel,[2] the silence had become heavy. Had the time of the end come? Would they speak again? The expectation was strong, because the presence of prophets was the sign that God was drawing near and visiting God's people. Consequently, Mary, the one "full of grace," fulfilled Israel's hopes.

Her role as prophetess, however, goes beyond anything that the ancient prophets could have envisioned. Indeed, Mary is charged with believing, attesting, and bearing witness that this child, similar to others except for sin, is the *God who comes.* In conjunction with the Spirit, she is the active agent of this prodigious translation of the things of God and heaven to the here below of human beings and the earth. The beyond has become close. From now on, all the gestures and common events of a human life will be illuminated from within by the divinity of this man. For it is to the Son of God that Mary will learn to speak; it is the Son of God that she will take in her arms to spare him the stones and the brambles. From now on, the word of God has a name that can be pronounced, a smell, a voice, a look; God has taken flesh. Mary has truly received the mystery in her inmost being, and it is she who, during the years in which she educated her son, has known its greatest amplitude, going from the total human to the total God, "without confusion or separation." This is why no one has possessed the gift of prophecy to this extent. No one has had the chance to deliver such a message.

Another major trait calls for some remarks. At the moment when Mary "gave birth to her firstborn son and wrapped him in bands of cloth, and laid him in a manger, because there was no place for them in the inn" (Luke 2:7), she had to discover, then prepare herself to announce a God who ran counter to the images of all-powerfulness that she would hold from her familiarity with the First Testament.

In the straw of the manger, there was only a God of weakness to contemplate. An infant is the absolute of fragility, of dependence, of surrendering oneself to others. How can we understand that this child to whom the angel of the annunciation gives the name of Jesus (Luke 1:31), "Savior" or "God saves," bring salvation? How do fragility and dependence save? Understanding it requires a radical detour; we must admit that Christ is savior because he obliges each one to come to the "help" of his neighbor. By helping, I help myself. On condition that I do not take pride in this mission, on condition that I almost do not realize it, I save myself from closing in on myself, I enrich myself with others. This is one of the major characteristics of the Jewish and Christian proposal. It affirms that salvation comes from the mutual help that human beings give one another. Let us remember that this is the first instruction given by the Creator to the first couple: that each one help the other. Closer to us, it is also the testimony of Etty Hillesum who, confronted with Nazi barbarity, ended up offering her life in solidarity with her Jewish brothers and sisters. She extends the instruction well beyond people to God. "One thing, however, appears more and more clear to me," she said to the Lord. "It is not you who can help us, but we who can help you and, in so doing, help ourselves."[3]

Mary the prophetess is also charged with this mission. When she sings in the Magnificat that "the Mighty One has done great things" for her (Luke 1:49), she knows what she is talking about. It takes a great deal of power to succeed in instilling in human beings the coming of a God of weakness, as far removed from the desire for power that inhabits them and from the usual conceptions of the divine.

MARY, "SPOKESWOMAN"

As a prophetess, Mary becomes the "spokeswoman" of God. The expression goes further than one might think. While the prophets of Israel listen to the oracles of the Most High, write them down on papyrus, and *carry* them by calling them "the word of God," Mary, for her part, *carries* a child. Her oracles, her word, is Jesus, the fulfillment of the "word of God." John explains it in his Prologue: "The Word [in Greek *logos*] became flesh" (John 1:14). In the strongest sense of the term, Mary bears the flesh of God. She is the "spokeswoman" of the entire Bible; she is its unsurpassed model.

If we follow the metaphor to its conclusion, we observe that, on the one hand, Mary carries a child who sums up all the scriptures, and on the other, John announces that the scriptures are taking flesh. Certainly, the scriptures have always had this bodily consistency, because they tell the story of the life of a people, but with Jesus, this "life" of the scriptures is embodied in a palpable, present, and exceptional human life. Knowing this, we cannot make the Bible a worn-out or obsolete book. The Bible is alive.

Mary, the one who gives birth to "the flesh of the scriptures" has a special relationship with the Torah, to the point that when opening the New Testament, the reader is never far away, through and with Mary, the "mother of the child-Word" of all scripture. Who better than she can invite us to see the presence of her son in the Bible? Not a material presence, but the culmination, in Jesus, of the great biblical themes: the denunciation of all servitude, the vocation of freedom, an unbreakable covenant of God with humanity, concern for the poor, trust in God, the desire to follow God's commandments even if they sometimes require transgressing the social order. All these themes are expressed in the Magnificat in which Mary deciphers and comments in advance on the message of her son. We have observed how, by her whole attitude and by her words, she is the hand that opens the Book, the finger that points to it. This is why, when painters or sculptors represent Mary with her child in her arms, they do not only show the tender image of a playful child and a mother radiating happiness. In the background of this family painting, we can see the culmination of the biblical work, its accomplishment, the Word made flesh.

Extending this idea, we can say that the birth of this child is not complete. Each time we open the Bible, Mary gives birth to her son again, and Jesus takes flesh for the reader. By this unique, exceptional quality of having given birth to the awaited Messiah, Mary is a prophet among prophets. None will have been closer to the message than she. If Mary is fully human, she is also the mother of a child whom she loves and raises with the affection he needs.

The reader, concerned about good relations between parents and their children, is entitled to ask how Jesus regards his mother. Are their exchanges affectionate, tender, or at least in conformity with the commandment of the Decalogue that asks us to honor our father and mother (Exod 20:12)? However, nothing in the Gospel account authorizes us to answer yes. We have already seen that Jesus disrupts parental relationships to put them at the service of God.[4] But he goes even further. With all due respect to Marian devotees, we must recognize that he is totally devoid of any Marian veneration.

Unfit, rebellious even! Not only do his words not think much of his mother, but worse still, all the circumstances recounted in the Gospels show him busy distancing himself from her. Thus, we have already noted that at the age of twelve, he vehemently denies that he owes her anything, to the point that she suffers (see Luke 2:41–50). Another time, Jesus's family, including his mother, want to see him, probably because a disagreement has arisen between his family and him over the direction he is taking. But Jesus rebels and evades them, even refusing to meet them, if this is how the silence of the text should be interpreted (see Mark 3:31–35; Matt 12:46–50; Luke 8:19–21).

Finally, at the foot of the cross, Jesus marks a final departure from his mother by giving her another son in the person of the beloved disciple (John 19:26–27). How could we, modern readers, not be unnerved by the harshness of such distancing?

Perhaps it was already from this perspective that Saint Ignatius of Loyola, not being consoled that a resurrected son did not go first to greet his mother, had imagined that Jesus had appeared to her, just for her.[5] The reason for this laconicism, then this erasure, can perhaps be explained by the fact that the evangelists are less sensitive than we modern people to the affective dimension of the relationships between parents and children. They want to edify readers so that their life with God grows. The absence of Mary at the resurrection confirms that the Gospels are not romantic stories and that they open up a space for the reader's involvement. It is thanks to this critical distance from historically situated—therefore, unreproducible—affective relationships that readers' own experience of the Gospels can begin. But Mary's absence at the resurrection also says that at that moment, theologically, her presence is no longer necessary. As we will soon see, at the foot of the cross, everything that was to be said between Jesus and his mother had already been said.

MARY, FULLY HUMAN

Mary was the first to be confronted with this mystery of the dual nature of Jesus, which would have to marinate for four centuries before it could be put into words. However, we must never forget that Mary is inserted into ordinary humanity. She raises a child who, in all likelihood, behaved like all children: who learned sociability like everyone else, who made mistakes and corrected himself, and who gradually settled into the bed of his human experiences. When we say that Jesus is without sin, we must understand it in its theological dimension: The link with God, his Father, exists in him. But he could very well have gone and stolen grapes from the vine or poured out his anger when his mother put him to bed too early. Mary is a witness to all this because she is his mother, present at his side.

Sacred history has too often mistreated Mary's humanity, both on the side of popular piety, which exalted her as quasi-divine, and by the later Marian dogmas that contribute to removing her from an ordinary humanity (conceived without sin and endowed with a body that knows no corruption). Because of both, and according to logic that is sometimes convergent, sometimes opposed, the story of Mary has become "a product" conforming to the expectations of a certain public. In the holy Catholic Church, the method has already proven itself. The most tragic example of this remodeling is that of Judas, demonized by the fathers to the point of serving as the basis for a Christian anti-Judaism. Just as it was necessary to reintegrate Judas into common humanity, made of shadows and light, it is also important to return Mary to common humanity. At the same time, this assignment is unlike any other, because it requires never losing sight of the mystery of the God-man she brought into the world. Mary knew how to keep her eyes open before a disconcerting child, who from childhood impressed the doctors of the law, a man opposed by his own family and then by the temple to the point of dying, who was both "like the others and different from them."

This insistence on Mary's ordinary relationships with her son in no way prevents her from also being the figure of Israel. On the contrary, by restoring her humanity, these two combined traits make Mary's a voice that everyone can hear, wherever they are. Similarly, when Paul in Galatians or Jesus in the Gospel of John soberly speak of her as "woman" (Gal 4:4; John 19:26), the anonymity of the expression speaks at once of the singularity of her person and the universality that it implies. Thus, everyone can be "the woman" who gives birth to Jesus. The major consequence is that God can inhabit a human conscience. This is what Saint Augustine will say: "Late have I loved you, Beauty so ancient and so new, late have I loved you. It is because you were within and I was outside of myself! And it is there that I sought you."[6] The believer is "theophoric": He or she "carries God." Such is "the good news according to Mary" from which each and all benefit. To verify this, we hardly need to wait for the words of Jesus: "Where two or three are gathered in my name, I am there among them" (Matt 18:20). Mary elevates the young daughter of Israel to the rank of a humanity which, collectively, is *capax Dei*, capable of God. What fertility in this birth!

All that we have just said places Mary at the center of the debates on the nature of Jesus, true God and true man. It must be recognized that this affirmation is unbearable if we relate it to the usual conceptions of God in most religions. From the incarnation to the crucifixion, the Jews found the adventure scandalous, and the Greeks considered it crazy (1 Cor 1:23). Many Christian heresies have defined themselves by opposing the idea that a woman is capable of giving birth to a god. Thus, in the second century, Marcion, disowned by the young Church for all that he rejects of the God of the Jews, could not bear that the divine dignity could accommodate itself to being born. With beautiful conviction, revealing the unease, Tertullian answered him:

> Describe to us then this belly, more monstrous from day to day, heavy, tormented, and never at rest, even in sleep, solicited on both sides by the whims of appetite and disgust. Now unleash yourself against the indecent organs of the woman in labor which nevertheless honor her by the danger she runs and which are naturally sacred. Apparently, he frightens you, this child rejected with weapons and baggage, and whom

> you disdain once again, washed, because it is necessary to keep him in swaddling clothes, knead him with ointments and make him laugh with caresses. You despise him, Marcion, this natural object of veneration: and how were you born? You hate the birth of man: and how can you then love someone?...Christ, at least, loved this man, this clot formed in the breast among the filth.[7]

Mary was the first to love this child-God formed in the womb and in the blood. She lived from this mystery.

IN THE SERVICE OF HER SON

Mary's prophetic mission is clear, as we have already mentioned: She is always to announce her Son, always to be devoted to him. This service begins on the first day of her pregnancy, as suggested by the words of Paul, already quoted "when the fullness of time had come, God sent his Son, born of a woman" (Gal 4:4). Fullness is what governs the life of a pregnant woman as she awaits her term. Every pregnant woman "waits." It is even a way of designating her. And the "times fulfilled" in fullness are the term. All mothers know that this term inaugurates the beginning of a companionship that will have no end. When a child is born, "times open" and every mother projects herself into the future. In a year, in twenty years, what will this infant have become? The birth of Jesus, Son of God, is the figure of the "liberation of times." The formula carries far. Mary experiences a pregnancy that takes her far beyond any human gestation, until the end of time that Christ inaugurates. She is the first to encounter this spiritual reality.

But there is more. Long before the great Pauline hymns—those in the Letter to the Ephesians (for example, Eph 1:3–14) and the hymn to the Colossians, which both represent the existence of the Word of God—Mary had to accept—even conceive!—that this child, whom she had received in her womb, had always preexisted in God. If mothers wonder where their child comes from, from what improbable combination of cells he or she emerged, why it is this child and not someone else, Mary had to learn to answer: "He has always been in God." According to the hymn to the Colossians, Christ is

> the firstborn of all creation; for in him all things in heaven and on earth were created, things visible and invisible, whether thrones or dominions or rulers or powers—all things have been created through him and for him. He himself is before all things, and in him all things hold together. (Col 1:15–17)

Theologian Joseph Moingt suggests that this preexistence is a *proexistence*. He thus suggests that Christ is ahead of us, that he walks ahead, leading the universe in his wake and giving meaning to all things. This antecedence invites everyone into relationship. The illustration of this idea would be the cloud that guided the people when they crossed the desert, which stopped above the chosen camp and rose when they had to set out (Exod 40:36–38). If Christ is "before us," he is "with us" and therefore "for us," to accomplish the loving project of his Father. It is to this very speculative but strong vision that the angel invited Mary. The preexistence of her son can mean that he is "preexistent," ahead of her, that he precedes her like the cloud. To this type of presence with Christ, the believer is also invited.

This closeness of Mary signals the great difference between her and John the Baptist, the prophet who comes to us from the scriptures. John is there to attest that Jesus is indeed the one we were waiting for, that there is no more waiting, that the times are fulfilled. Once his mission is accomplished, the Baptist can disappear. Mary, however, is situated differently: She must always be there, as an emissary of humanity contemplating the one who will have no end. Moreover, the evangelists do not give any information about her at the end of their writings. Thus, Mary never "leaves" their stories. Mary must also hear and accept the announcement that a sword will pierce her heart (Luke 2:35). This child that Mary welcomes is a God whose passion and indirectly whose resurrection have been announced.

This tension inserted a few verses apart, between the glory of bearing God and the pain of the cross, is perhaps the place in which two ways of speaking of Christ, two Christologies, are held together: the classical "high Christology," and "low Christology," which is closer, no doubt, to what the first disciples perceived and is more accessible to contemporary minds. In the first, in the incarnation, the Son of God comes into the world; in the second, the resurrection makes us understand that Jesus is the Son of God.

High Christology takes form in the angel's announcement: "And now, you will conceive in your womb and bear a son, and you will name him Jesus. He will be great, and will be called the Son of the Most High, and the Lord God will give him the throne of his ancestor David. He will reign over the house of Jacob forever, and of his kingdom there will be no end" (Luke 1:31–33). The titles given to her son allow us to attribute to Mary, in the fourth century, her qualification of "Mother of God." Low Christology is clearly expressed in Peter's speech on the day of Pentecost. "This man, handed over to you according to the definite plan and foreknowledge of God, you crucified and killed by the hands of those outside the law. But God raised him up....Being therefore exalted at the right hand of God, and having received from the Father the promise of the Holy Spirit, he has poured out this" (Acts 2:23–24a, 33). Mary resolutely holds both. With her, we discover the depth of a mystery that can tear apart, but that a life of faith teaches us to unite.

Thus, this chapter, by insisting on the common humanity of Mary, also brought out the exceptional character of her mission. Jean-Paul Sartre, in an astonishing meditation written in 1940 in a prison camp, summarizes her mission here:

> And it is a hard test for a mother to be ashamed of herself and her human condition in front of her son. But I think that there are also other quick and slippery moments when she feels at the same time that Christ is her son, her little one, and that he is God. She looks at him and she thinks: "This God is my child. This divine flesh is my flesh. He is made of me,...he is God and he resembles me." And no woman has had her God like that all to herself. A tiny God whom one can take in

> one's arms and cover with kisses, a warm God who smiles and breathes, a God whom one can touch and who lives.[8]

A prophetess of an unheard-of kind, a "bearer of the Word," Mary brought things from heaven down to earth. She is a sure guide for those who want to know God made man. This portrait must now be completed by a close analysis of the unique motherhood that Mary experiences, both as mother of Jesus and mother of Christ.

10

MARY, MOTHER OF JESUS

AFTER TRYING TO shed light on the membership of Mary in common humanity, we can return to the title "mother," which naturally comes to mind when speaking of her. We have already devoted a chapter to showing how Mary's motherhood, not being comparable to others, prohibits making her a model for women. After having highlighted what she is not, let us dwell on what she is. We will look at her exceptional motherhood that is told in the light of theology and, as always, we will look at Mary in the New Testament. Each mention deserves to be noted and placed in its context. It is often the latter that will reveal its scope. This is demanding work, not without setbacks, but so fruitful that it deserves the two chapters to come. The first will shed light on Mary's contribution to the humanity of Jesus, and the next will focus on his divinity. The first will focus on Paul, Mark, and Matthew, the second on John and Luke–Acts. This division is useful provided that it is not rigid, because all the writers are obviously imbued with the certainty of the human-divine nature of Jesus. But since they are addressing potentially different audiences and were not all written at the same time, their nuances are different. Thus, when an evangelist insists on the humanity of Jesus, he does not forget his divinity: "He whom I believe to be God, I must constantly be reminded that he is a man." And conversely: "This man apparently like everyone else, I will show is also the Christ sent from the Father." This tension demands that we never lose sight of the presuppositions or implications of the evangelists.

THE RETICENCE OF PAUL AND MARK

Let us recall once again the short and unique statement by which Paul, chronologically the first New Testament writer, announces the birth of Jesus. He was "born of a woman" (Gal 4:4). This economy of information is surprising because it is both too obvious and not precise enough, but it is crucial. Without naming Mary, Paul shows that the "matrix of Jesus" is common humanity, starting from the reality of a pregnancy.

Jesus is fully human, and ordinary humanity was able to engender him. This is Paul's message through this formula, as chiseled as it is effective. His observation will be important in countering Docetism, the heresy that appeared very early and that denies the full humanity of Christ. We have seen that for the Docetists, if the Word "became" flesh, Jesus would nevertheless not be an ordinary human being. He could not suffer, nor live in a body similar to that of all humans, and his death on the cross could not lead to the common fate of annihilation.

Docetism is a serious doctrinal deviation that was fought vigorously. Saint Irenaeus, a great slayer of heresies, draws on this text from Paul to develop his analysis of the role of Mary.

Paul's great reticence when it comes to evoking the figure of Mary is also found in the Gospel of Mark. This has not escaped the attention of biblical scholar Charles Perrot. He points out what seems to be reluctance on the part of these two authors and notes that if "women are largely highlighted in his writing [in Mark], Mary hardly is."[1] He recalls that Mark is part of the Pauline line and suggests a historical explanation. The family of Jesus—Mary, but also his brothers, including James of Jerusalem, "the brother of the Lord"—belong to the clan that opposes Paul. Moreover, Paul, in his Letter to the Galatians, speaks of "certain people...from James" (Gal 2:12) in a less than complimentary manner.

This confrontation between "churches" would perhaps be an explanation for the silence of the Apostle. But it is also possible that the concerns of the first disciples were less about the biography of Jesus than about his message. The writings of Paul and Mark are the first in the New Testament, and they are primarily intended to announce the Son of God the Savior.

Charles Perrot highlights the diversity of the names of Mary, which is linked to the various currents of the first century.[2] For Luke, Mary is "a virgin named Mary,"[3] while in John, she is designated more soberly as "the mother of Jesus," never evoked by her virginity. Finally, she is "the mother of the Messiah" in the churches born from Jewish communities and in the Gospel of Matthew.

But Mark's contribution is not only manifested by silence. The verse where Mary's name appears for the only time will amply demonstrate it: "Is not this the carpenter, the son of Mary and brother of James and of Joses and Judas and Simon?" (Mark 6:3). Mark places him in an ordinary family context, surrounded by his siblings. And it is interesting to note that, contrary to the custom that refers to the son by way of his father, calling him "son of...," Mark does not say "son of Mary and Joseph" but only "son of Mary." For Mark as for Paul, Mary, inserted in common human relations, guarantees the humanity of Jesus.

Now let us observe which evangelists speak more about it.

IN MATTHEW, MARY'S POWER OF PROCREATION

We have already commented on the Gospel of Matthew concerning the four women of Jesus's lineage and the virginity of Mary. Let us recall that one of the purposes of this genealogy is to say that Jesus is "of the line of David," thus to prepare for his title of "Messiah," descendant of David for whom Israel was waiting. Let us now undertake a more systematic review of the mentions he makes of Mary's motherhood. In the genealogy the "social heredity" of Jesus is thus mentioned: "Jacob the father of

Joseph *the husband of Mary*, of whom Jesus was born, who is called the Messiah."

What Is Mary Called in the New Testament?

This table summarizes the titles given to Mary. It emerges that the term by which she is most often referred to is her title of mother, followed by her first name. On the other hand, the term *virgin*, so commonly given to Mary today, only appears to introduce her.

"**Family of Jesus**": Mark 3:31–35
"**His own**": Mark 3:20–21
"**Mary**": Matt 1:16, 18, 20; 2:11; Mark 6:3; Luke 1:30, 34, 38, 39, 41, 46, 56; Luke 2:5, 19, 33; Acts1:14 (16 references).
"The **mother**," "His mother," "Mother of Jesus": Matt 1:18; 2:11, 13, 14, 20, 21; Luke 1:43; 2:48, 51; John 2: 1, 3, 5, 12; 19:25, 26, 27; Acts 1:14 (17 references)
"The **virgin**": Matt 1:23; "A virgin betrothed," "The virgin's name was Mary": Luke 1:27 (3 references)
A **woman**," "Woman," "Your **wife**," "His wife": Gal 4:4; Matt 1: 20, 24; John 2:4; 19:26 (6 references)

Commentators pay little attention to this last term, which presents the roles in reverse of all the social conventions of the time: It is not Mary who is Joseph's wife, but it is Joseph who is mentioned as the "husband of Mary" in a hierarchical reversal that immediately signals the important character of the couple. It recalls what we have already noted in the text of Mark when it invokes the "son of Mary."

After this genealogy, Matthew presents Mary through her relationship to Jesus: "The birth of Jesus the Messiah took place in this way. When his mother Mary had been engaged to Joseph" (Matt 1:18). And the writer announces an event that seems like an interruption: "Before they lived together, she was found to be with child" (Matt 1:19). He will describe the rest from Joseph's point of view since, socially, it is on him that the action rests. This particular "father" will have the essential responsibility of transmitting his Davidic filiation to the child, by giving him his name and, as the rest of the story confirms, he will raise him as his son.

However, Mary does not have a minor role. By verse 19 indicating her pregnancy, she has come to fulfill the promise announced by Isaiah, which Matthew quotes: "Therefore the Lord himself will give you a sign. Look, the young woman is with child and shall bear a son, and shall name him Immanuel" (Isa 7:14).

Thus, Matthew privileges the position of Mary as the mother of Jesus. He mentions her intervention in the fulfillment of the promise—she will be the mother of Immanuel ("God with us")—and he anchors her motherhood in the messianic genealogy by linking her to Joseph. Then, in order to establish the seriousness of this adventure, Matthew, throughout his story, leaves Joseph in the role of the main character. It is to him that the angel appears, first to reassure him of his paternity: "Do not be afraid to take Mary as your wife, for the child conceived in her is from the Holy Spirit" (Matt 1:20), then, after the birth of the child, to encourage him to return from Egypt, where fear of Herod had made them flee: "An angel of the Lord suddenly appeared in a dream to Joseph in Egypt and said, 'Get up, take the child and his mother, and go to the land of Israel, for those who were seeking the child's life are dead'" (Matt 2:19). The "flight into Egypt," which has inspired many artists, and the return to Israel that followed allows Jesus and his parents to "ascend" from the place of slavery, Egypt, to the promised land. The savior, like the people of Israel from which he came, has known the servitude of all people, and he is freed from it by the angel of the Lord—that is, by the Lord himself—whom his parents obey. With this episode, Joseph places Jesus in the history of Israel.

Matthew's story would then seem to confine Mary to a maternal function, understood in a passive way. Moreover, Mary is only mentioned four times by name in this Gospel and always in reference to her motherhood. Everything would therefore lead to underestimating her role. But there is this final verse of the genealogy already mentioned in which Matthew recognizes in Mary, and in her alone, the power to engender Jesus, specifying just after the genealogy that she was pregnant "from the Holy Spirit." This mention is the "bridge" that connects Mary to the other women of the genealogy of her son and indicates the choice of God; the reader will then be able to suppose that the Spirit incites this transgression of the rules for the benefit of accomplishing the Word when the kings and the priests no longer know how to transmit it. The whole sequence leads the reader to deduce that Mary has the power of engendering while Joseph guarantees the Davidic and royal lineage of the Messiah.

Mary hardly appears again in this Gospel except to serve as a framework for a definition of the "true family of Jesus" (Matt 12:46–50). The restraint with which this mother is not distinguished from the rest of her relatives highlights, first of all, the choice of an environment of election rather than of blood. However, the mention of this family to which Jesus belongs makes him a totally human being that the inflation of his divinity sometimes sought to mask in the early days of Christianity. Still, the continuous theological approach up until the Council of Chalcedon aimed to affirm faith in a Christ who was both man and God.

In Matthew, the presence of Jesus's brothers also underlines the incarnate character of this family and disqualifies certain discourses on Mary that would make her a being out of touch with reality. She is part of the cultural and social framework of her time, subverting it if necessary. It is tricky to translate *adelphoï sou* other than by "your brothers"[4] because doing so would deny Joseph's wife the place of wife and mother, which were the roles of every woman in Israel. The following verses accredit this "normality" of Jesus's family circle by speaking again of his mother and his siblings: "Is this not the carpenter's son? Is not his mother called Mary? And are not his brothers James and Joseph and Simon and Judas? And are not all his sisters with us?" (Matt 13:55–56). Mary's motherhood does not take her outside the ordinary field of a couple's married life and interpersonal relationships.

There are thus two ways of presenting Mary from this Gospel. Either we maintain the traditional version, which paints the portrait of a self-effacing, silent woman, since not a word of hers is reported, who remains at a distance from the actions of the divine son that the Spirit gave her. Or we measure all that it must have cost a reporter such as Matthew, very steeped in the traditions of his country, to recognize the elements that we have underlined. They make Mary the principal vector of the coming of Jesus into the world. Through her the announcement of Isaiah is fulfilled, that of the coming of Immanuel. In this second perspective, Joseph is no more than her husband. Mary assures both the humanity of her son and his divinity by engendering him through the action of the Spirit. This picture presents Jesus according to three perspectives: He is divine, because he was engendered by the Spirit; he is in continuity with the First Testament, because Mary is the young girl described by Isaiah; and he is fully human, because Mary assumes the ordinary place of a mother.

Let us then discover how the Gospel of John, from another perspective, gives Mary a decisive place in the plan of salvation.

11

MARY, MOTHER OF CHRIST

IF MARY IS "mother of Jesus," she is also "mother of Christ," as underlined by the title of this new chapter devoted to Mary's motherhood. The Gospel of John, written later than the Synoptics (Matthew, Mark, and Luke, which can be compared in parallel, hence their name "Synoptics"), does not give us the details of Luke and Matthew on the birth and childhood of Jesus, nor on the virginity of Mary. Yet we will discover that Mary plays a significant role, suggested in a few remarkably brief sentences that highlight both Mary's theological role and the author's ability to suggest a lot with very little. At the wedding at Cana (John 2:1–12) and at the passion (John 19:26–27), Mary is present. In these two places, the beginning and end of Jesus's preaching, she will collaborate decisively in the mission of her son. She appears here, more than in other Gospels, as the "mother of Christ."

INCREDIBLE AUDACITY

The story of the wedding at Cana is essential in John's project, because it reveals all of the Gospel's theological axes and subtly prepares the reader for the scene of the crucifixion.

Let us enter the story. "On the third day there was a wedding in Cana of Galilee" (2:1). The mention of the "third day" reminds Bible readers of the time of God's manifestation in the desert when he concluded the covenant with his people: "on the third day the Lord will come down upon Mount Sinai in the sight of all the people" (Exod 19:11b). Of course, this mention also refers to another third day to come, that of the resurrection.

If the date is rich in symbols, what can we say about the setting? The scene does not take place in the temple, nor even in Jerusalem. We are in a place neither of power nor of great human population. On the contrary, we are in a small town in Galilee, a province rather poorly regarded by the Judeans because it welcomes mixed populations, and in a locality of which the Bible hardly speaks. A curious place for someone who would like to manifest his glory! In this place, the reader is transported to the heart of a wedding, an opportunity for gathering in joy, the joy of a covenant between two spouses that recalls the covenant in the desert between the people and God, to which John has just alluded by the mention of the "third day."

The protagonists of the story are soon mentioned: "And the mother of Jesus was there. Jesus and his disciples had also been invited" (2:1b–2). Let us note that it is Mary who is invited, and her son Jesus who accompanies her. She is therefore, more than Jesus, "in her milieu," her natural and privileged place of action. Already, in Matthew, Mary was in the central place, Joseph being presented in reference to her as her husband. The following scene, decisive and well-known, is this: "The mother of Jesus said to him: 'They have no wine.' And Jesus said to her, 'Woman, what concern is that to you and to me? My hour has not yet come.' His mother said to the servants, 'Do whatever he tells you'" (2:3–5).

In this short dialogue, the first sentence is already intriguing. It is Mary who begins the dialogue and, by pointing out the lack of wine, sets the *pace*. Will Jesus leave the guests without the wedding wine? The choice of words draws our attention because she says: "They have no *wine*," where one would expect to hear: "They have no *more* wine." Does she not already suggest that it is not the wine of the vine that they lack, but "another wine" that only her son could give? The writer, as a good connoisseur of the scriptures, knows that each word opens up other readings. The words put into the mouths of Jesus and Mary take all their weight from the scripture that they call upon. The prophets have made familiar the image of the Lord, master of the vineyard, who invites Israel to the banquet of the end of time, and all human action aims to be worthy of taking part in that banquet. There, they will be regaled with the wine of the knowledge of God. Let us therefore take it for granted that the mother of Jesus is thinking of this precious wine and not of the simple wine of the banquet of Cana.

Now let us come to Jesus's answer to his mother. Among the profusion of comments prompted by their repartee, let us cite only that of Irenaeus who supposes that "the Lord rejects her untimely haste."[1] Is it simple haste that is in question here? Nothing tells us whether or not she knows that she is summoning her son to another plane that will lead him toward death. But it is obvious that Mary confronts Jesus with his mission in a radical way. Her son's reaction, close to denial, helps the reader understand that the moment is crucial. If Jesus rebels, he nevertheless announces that there is an "hour" toward which he is moving. The word is uttered; Mary has never heard it before. But it is her remark that has aroused him, by summoning her son to provide this missing wine. Now the subject is on the banquet table and can no longer be removed.

Where does this knowledge come from that made Mary capable of such audacity? What does she know of the divine mission of her son? In what way is he the "Christ" sent from the Father? In the context of the Gospel of John, Mary knows Jesus in two ways. The first is her experience as a mother, which is so obvious that it is not illustrated by the evangelist. Another source arises from the Prologue that John has placed at the beginning of his Gospel and that, for the sake of the literary exposition, Mary must know. The Prologue closes with a sentence that evokes a special kinship: "No one has ever seen God. It is God the only Son, who is close to the Father's heart, who has made him known" (John 1:18). This child comes from the *womb* of his mother, but he would also be in another *womb*,[2] that of his Father in heaven. If Mary, like each of the believers, cannot totally understand this paternity, she nevertheless sees her son under the prism of this major kinship with the Father, of which the Prologue says that it exists since "the beginning."

Through this double knowledge, Mary is capable of taking a considerable risk, that of pointing out to Jesus that the guests have no wine. And she is right on target! If she had been mistaken, Jesus would have answered her: "Go and ask the master of the house, or the owner of the vineyard, but not me!" However, he recognizes that these words are addressed to him; the missing wine is therefore that which comes from God, and the mother of Jesus discovers, or confirms what she believes, that her son can do something about the reported lack. Finally, as a sign that Jesus feels affected, he immediately responds to this invitation with a sharp withdrawal that reflects his inner turmoil; "the hour" has not yet come. But Jesus cannot forget about it.

MARY, GUARDIAN OF THE "HOUR"

In the Gospel of John, "the hour" for Jesus is much more than a moment; it crystallizes his entire work. Later, Jesus will recognize that he has come to "the hour" (John 12:27), the summit of his mission, the moment of revelation of "heavenly things" (John 3:12), as he will say to Nicodemus in the following chapter. Jesus's denial proves that he knows the price attached to "the hour," because he will have to give another wine, his own blood, on the cross. Clearly, if the passion is "the moment," the hour covers what will happen there by the elevation on the cross: the "glorification of the Son," by the demonstration of the love given. At Cana, Mary brings about "the hour" by her remark: "They have no wine." She is, in a certain way, its anticipator and, as we will soon verify, she will remain its guardian.

But there is more. Her address to the servants redoubles her audacity: "Do whatever he tells you." The introduction of the servants into the story leads to a triangular relationship, intended to reinforce the request. Mary uses them as leverage to get her son to "enter into the hour." She makes them her allies. Note that Mary's remarks resemble those domino pieces that fall down one after the other after a start has been given. Finally, Mary gives this last word additional weight, by drawing it from scripture. It was spoken by Pharaoh in response to the starving Egyptian people who were crying out for bread: "Go to Joseph; what he says to you, do" (Gen 41:55). Indeed, Joseph, Jacob's son, had suggested to Pharaoh that he store the wheat from the good harvests to guard against future bad harvests. All Egypt had the gratitude of a full belly, despite being at risk of dying. Pharaoh's words thus evoke the boundless trust granted to the one who guarantees the saving of life. Here, the mother of Jesus confesses the trust she has in her son, capable of nourishing, in another way, those who will call upon him.

Jesus, unmasked by his mother, shaken by the boundless trust she shows him, will comply with her intervention. Let us look closely at the text. The jars in question are filled with water "for the Jewish rites of purification" (2:6). The purification rites, which were numerous in the Jewish religion, took place in the temple and in homes. In all cases, the prescriptions were managed by the priests of the temple, responsible for applying the law of Moses. With this information, John shows that Jesus is part of the Jewish tradition. He has not come "to abolish [the law] but to fulfill [it]" (Matt 5:17). Jesus will even know how to bring, through its transformation into wine, a new enthusiasm for the law in which Mary collaborates as an actor of the covenant. This water therefore provides a support for the realization of the "sign" that Jesus wants to give. Faced with all this information, the reader will have understood that the lack of wine is not caused by the improvidence of the inviting family. But rather, there is another level of reading that John, as a good writer, suggests without describing it. It is up to the reader in search of salvation to find it.

These six jars evoke the six days of creation that Christ comes to reorient in the history of salvation. They represent a considerable quantity of liquid: at least five hundred liters. Moreover, Jesus asks that they be filled with water, which the servants do scrupulously: "up to the brim," so as to satisfy all needs.

The rest of the story will describe how this water changed into wine "moves" each of the participants according to their way of welcoming the good news. Mary, who knows, is ahead of everyone; Jesus's companions, having seen, will believe; the servants and guests will have seen, but not understood. As for the chief steward of the meal, from a family friendly to Mary, it is not easy to qualify his reply (which by closing the story, gives some of its meaning). Is he a smooth talker who quibbles, like the doctors of the law, when he says to the bridegroom: "Everyone serves the good wine first, and then the inferior wine after the guests have become drunk"? Or, by complimenting the bridegroom: "But you have kept the good wine until now" (2:10), is he not in reality addressing Jesus, another bridegroom of another wedding described by the prophets, that of God with his people? And does not the "now" announce this other, imminent wedding? Even if we cannot decide, it is possible that this man recognizes the divinity of the bridegroom of Israel, Jesus. In that case, Mary, by her audacity, would have opened his eyes.

All these observations confirm that Mary knows that her son is not only human, but also the Son of God. Whether as a mother or more symbolically as a "figure of Israel," she has sensed that the people of God are lacking something more essential than the water of purification. They are lacking the wine that leads to the kingdom and already signifies its presence. She echoes the distress of a people awaiting the fulfillment of the eschatological wedding announced by the prophets. The conclusion of the story shows how the expectations of Israel and the plan of divine salvation come together without it being possible to disentangle the one from the other: "Jesus did this, the first of his signs...and revealed his glory; and his disciples believed in him" (2:11).

At Cana, Mary's request is crucial, because it brings about the hour that Jesus did not consider had yet come. Let us recall that John does not recount the baptism of Jesus, as Matthew does. The reader is entitled to consider that Cana, this moment when Mary "immersed" her son in his public ministry, is a baptism for Jesus. Thus, from this wedding, the good news is told and can be told again. Through the wine offered, the covenant with a God who becomes human will be renewed, to lead the believer to the Father in order to "divinize" him. By sharing the wine, Christ Jesus already invites everyone to the feast of the resurrection.

Let us remember that Mary, here given the title of "mother," acts as such. The trust that mothers instill in their children is a *topos* of emotional life. Mary, strong in her experience of motherhood, conscious of the power that it gives her, shows her absolute faith in her son. Thus, she teaches everyone how to arouse in others their capacity to create, to "reveal" themselves, despite their possible resistance. We are witnessing a new birth, a childbirth. But this second childbirth does not end at Cana. Mary's *work* will last, without the stages being signified, until the foot of the cross, where we will find her again.

AT THE FOOT OF THE CROSS

It is logical to find Mary at the cross when "the hour has come." Moreover, she will be invested with the message of bringing about "the hour" after the death of Jesus, and this forever. Let us first recall that at the foot of the cross, in the Synoptics as in John, several women, including Mary, are "witnesses," in the evangelical sense of the word. They do not simply verify that the man Jesus is indeed dead—although it is important to certify this—but they support with their presence and compassion the suffering and agony of their son and friend. They accompany him to the end. Their fidelity is one of the most poignant there is. Loving someone who is disfigured, who no longer has any future, who will never again render you any service, is the very definition of love.

The specific presence in this place of "the mother of Jesus" is mentioned only in John, in a brief message that mutually entrusts Mary and the disciple whom Jesus loves to each other: "'Woman, here is your son.' Then he [Jesus] said to the disciple, 'Here is your mother'" (John 19:26–27). It is in this command that Jesus delivers the last message of his testament, even if he will then pronounce a final word: "I am thirsty." And John makes his readers understand that Jesus will be obeyed: "From that hour the disciple took her into his own home" (19:27).

Let us observe that this instruction does not pertain to the other women present. Why? John thus emphasizes that Mary is the recipient of a particular message, linked to her identity. This short dialogue is, like that of Cana, of fundamental importance. It initiates new links, of another order, between Mary and the disciple, as well as between those they represent. Because he is *unnamed*, without a precise identity, the "beloved" to whom Jesus entrusts his mother leaves room for any disciple, according to this law of literature which identifies the reader with him. Thus, Jesus integrates the entire community into the heart of this new type of birth. All can become brothers and sisters, daughters and sons of Mary, from whom Jesus detached himself by calling her "woman." Here too, this trait deserves our attention: Jesus is on the threshold of his death, he manifests his autonomy, or rather his difference, by subtly untying the ties that connect him to his mother, as if it were a question of freeing her from an emotional hold that was too strong.

Apocalypse, Eschatology...

The expression "from that hour" is, in Jewish and Christian thought, much less banal than it seems. It means that the last times have come.

Jewish religious thought has given much reflection to the question of the end of time. It has even invented a literary genre, "apocalyptic," centered on the coming of God at the end of time. This word, which means "revelation," is far from the current common meaning, that of a catastrophe.

Early Christianity took up the theme, frequently announcing "the return of the Lord." The first Christians were in the habit of greeting or parting by saying: *marana tha*, "the Lord is coming" (Rev 22:20 and 1 Cor 16:22). This invitation is not to be interpreted in a material sense, but in a theological sense, although any construction of this type is anchored in a history. Believing that the Lord will come is simply the consequence of faith. And according to Jewish and Christian thought, these times are still ours. The "last times" are simply those in which the Christian lives.

Why, then, this dramatization that could seem artificial, and therefore suspect? For the first Christians, this expression sensitizes the interlocutor to the presence of God and to the ethical consequences of the coming of Jesus. From now on, love obliges. Mary, welcomed "from that hour," is the tutelary figure who accompanies the life of a believer during these last times.

Of course, Jesus does not ask the disciple to prepare a room to welcome Mary into his home after his death, although an explanation of this type remains to be considered: Those who assisted the crucified, considered bandits, were liable to be punished, which shows that the women who came to the foot of the cross were not only faithful, but courageous. Should the "beloved" protect Mary? But then, why would the evangelist not take the other three women present under his roof? Everything indicates rather that we are in a different register than that of the materiality of the facts. Jesus's instruction concerns the future, after his departure. In scholarly terms, one would say that it is "eschatological."

Note that the Greek text says "*the* mother" and not "his mother," contrary to what almost all Bibles translate.[3] The biblical scholar Jean-Pierre Lémonon observes that this detail is not unique.[4] To demonstrate this, he refers to Isaiah[5] who makes Jerusalem the "messianic community," a mother who gives birth to many children. John places Mary in this continuity. "Mother of Israel," she is also called to give birth to many other children. This reminder allows us to better qualify the relationships between the Jewish world and the young Judeo-Christian communities that were emerging in the Roman world, at the time when John was writing. He is concerned to show that the coherence of the Christian message comes from its anchor in the scriptures, therefore in the people of Israel, chosen by God. "The mother," from this perspective, is Mary, the one who spreads her cloak at the same time over Israel and over Christians. As Luke showed, who himself relied on the motherhood of Israel, John makes Mary "the Mother" who offers the scriptures to all the beloved disciples who will come, and also the one who will remain the symbolic mother of Israel in comparison to future disciples who will not be Jewish. It follows that a responsibility toward Israel remains, and it is Mary who represents it and assumes it. She remains, while John the Baptist disappears.[6] Beyond the persecution fomented against Israel by Herod after Jesus's birth,[7] Mary as Israel will grant hospitality to the disciple, the outline of a new community that will have Israel as its mother. The Christian responsibility toward Israel finds its origin here.

This same episode takes us even further. Jesus gives Mary as mother to the disciple. Mother of a unique motherhood that is not limited to its carnal dimension, mother qualified as "woman," which accentuates the distance with her biological reality, Mary becomes a participant in the community of disciples.

It is also the future community whose place is outlined here. "From this hour," says John. A relay is set up to take over the continuation of the "hour," which becomes imminent since Jesus is going to "give up his spirit." Mary, whom we have already identified as the "guardian of the hour," will persevere in this mission. Another hour, a new countdown of time begins, for which the beloved disciple and Mary will be accountable. For them, time will unfold differently. Of course, behind the question of the hour, it is not time that is at stake. Mary and the Beloved open the way to the demand for love manifested by the glorification of Jesus. Jesus creates a definitive filiation between Mary and the beloved disciple, that is to say between every person, for all time. Here he establishes as a model the perfect community that refers to the first creation in which God creates the human in God's image: "man and woman." From this new creation, Mary and the disciple become the new figures.

These observations lead us to a radical conclusion concerning Mary. She is no longer a person situated in history, defined by her motherhood, but every woman, and even every human being. Max Thurian emphasizes that in this way: Jesus breaks the time of ordinary family ties. "[He] can no longer be considered the human son of Mary, and the Virgin has ceased her role as the human mother of God....Mary must pass from her function as mother of Jesus to that of woman in the Church."[8] The first communities believed in the imminence of the end of time.[9] The nascent Church, a human community of those who believe, saw in it its own foreshadowing.

Finally, we must note the almost absolute reciprocity between the two instructions: "Woman, here is your son" and "Here is your mother." Besides a distancing, this symbolic motherhood toward the beloved disciple, that is to say toward every member of the believing community, reveals two important realities. The first is the perfect reciprocity of the instruction, the strict symmetry of attitude of the two characters. There is no longer any question of biological filial relationship or adoption. They are equal in future community responsibility. The second reality is contained in the instruction given to Mary. How will a member of the community be a "mother" if not through biology or adoption? Referring to the original plan of the Creator will come to our aid.

7+7: A New Creation

The Gospel of John follows a strict construction intended to emphasize how much the coming of the Son of God is a new creation. The writer organizes his message on the theme of the seven days of creation (between John 1:19 and John 4:54). If he elaborates it in this way, it is not only to connect to the First Testament by copying it but to magnify the event that is announced in the Jewish religious landscape. Nothing less than the culmination of all of Israel's expectation! To do this, he places seven other days, counted from their terminus: the resurrection, a moment of re-creation and of new creation, comparable to the first. The stages are as follows:

1. The anointing at Bethany, "six days before the Passover" (12:1).
2. The entry into Jerusalem (12:12).
3. The washing of the feet (13:1ff.).
4. The arrest of Jesus (18:1).
5. The appearance before Caiaphas (18:24).
6. The preparation day, the day of Jesus's death (18:28).
7. The tomb found empty (20:1).

The episode we are commenting on is associated with the sixth day of re-creation. Linked to the imminence of the "hour" of Jesus, it is one of the "signs" of this Gospel. We have seen that it consists of the creation of the new community founded on Mary and the "beloved" disciple, a man and a woman, as if echoing the second chapter of Genesis. Strict equality, in natural fidelity to the story of creation (see Gen 2:18).

THE COMPLETE DISCIPLE

Finally, in Luke, Mary is the complete disciple. It remains for us to broaden our view of Mary's motherhood utilizing both of Luke's books. In his Gospel, when Jesus is not yet born, the two future mothers Elizabeth and Mary visit each other. During this "visitation," the child that Elizabeth is expecting leaps, and she is ecstatic: "And why has this happened to me, that the mother of my Lord comes to me?" (Luke 1:43). In this scene, the emphasis is on the ability given to John the Baptist, a figure from the First Testament,[10] to recognize Christ from the womb, and to his mother, Elizabeth, who also assumes this ability herself. With this evocation, Luke signifies that the Jewish scriptures welcome the coming of a messiah. Mary's child is indeed the one that the history of Israel awaits.

At the beginning of the Acts of the Apostles, Luke's second volume dedicated to the propagation of the good news of the resurrection from Jerusalem to Rome, the disciples are gathered "with certain women, including Mary the mother of Jesus, as well as his brothers" in the company of the Eleven (Acts 1:13–14).[11] Her name appears next to his brothers, at the end of the list of those present. She is not placed in the center, as we see in icons or on the canvases of Western artists. All are gathered to pray. Days later, at Pentecost, the first meeting of an ecclesial assembly is held, which could be compared to the birth of the Church. Mary is present without being expressly named. But she becomes above all a disciple among the disciples since, like the others, she receives the Spirit:

> When the day of Pentecost had come, they were all together in one place. And suddenly from heaven there came a sound like the rush of a violent wind, and it filled the entire house where they were sitting. Divided tongues, as of fire, appeared among them, and a tongue rested on each of them. All of them were filled with the Holy Spirit and began to speak in other languages, as the Spirit gave them ability. (Acts 2:1–4)

The feast of Pentecost exudes strong symbolism. It is an agricultural feast, the "Feast of the Ingathering," fifty days after Easter, where the renewal of the covenant is celebrated and, in a later tradition, the gift of the law. Luke orients the feast toward the gift of the Spirit, which Mary's participation guarantees. It is important for Luke that Mary, the figure of Israel, contributes to this renewal of the covenant. The opening toward a non-Jewish world will henceforth take place "under the covenant." But if Mary also welcomes the gift of the Spirit at Pentecost, let us remember that the Spirit had already come upon her (Luke 1:35). If she receives it again, is it not to attest to the establishment of a new covenant, which has become universal, and which comes to inaugurate, at the heart of the community, the time of the Church?

Thus, through these two chapters, two figures of Mary have emerged. They essentially come from two approaches to the mystery of Christ, depending on whether one privileges the coming of the Word, that is to say the birth of Jesus—his incarnation—or whether one emphasizes his human history—his death and his resurrection. We have said that the first schema obeys a high Christology, "from above," or "descending," evoked in this chapter, which follows the path of the coming to earth of the Son of the Father and his revelation to Israel. In this context, the role of Mary will have been to show Christ present in Jesus. This is the story that John and Luke tell. The other configuration is ordered according to a low Christology "from below," or "ascending,"[12] because the exemplary life of this man, enlightened by his passion, makes us understand that Jesus is the Son of God. In Paul, Matthew, and indirectly in Mark (see the previous chapter), we have seen that Mary was the guarantor of the real humanity of Jesus. As Bernard Sesboüé explains,[13] the complementarity of the two movements is necessary, but this theologian, like many of his contemporaries, places the center of gravity around the death-resurrection of Christ and not his birth.

This view is not neutral with regard to the place given to Mary, for, already, the believing reader privileges in theology and in heart one or the other of the portraits of Mary drawn by the reader's preferred Christology. If we observe Mary from the angle of the incarnation, it is the annunciation that takes the light. This figure of Mary, virgin mother and centered on the marvelous birth of her son, leads her to be a passive receptacle, then a mother of sorrows. On the other hand, by following an ascending

Christology that values the humanity of Jesus, the figure of his mother becomes that of a daring woman, a symbol of Zion, a committed and faithful disciple, on whom Christ chooses to found his Church at the moment of giving up his spirit. The Magnificat, Cana, and the "Upper Room" are then highlighted. Tradition has preserved four Gospels side by side. Two present the "Infancy Gospels"; the other two do not. This diversity of images invites us to the difficult exercise of holding both representations.

At the end of this close analysis of the texts, we have gathered a quantity of precious clues. As much as a superficial reading of the Bible disappoints, because nothing catches the mind, a meticulous reading offers a harvest of clues that, put end to end, take on meaning and open up perspectives of extreme richness. The reader feels the satisfaction of seeing that the questions that have been asked are well founded and have answers. Matthew has shown us a Mary who becomes a mother at the cost of a considerable social transgression. In the eyes of humans, she has lost her virginity; she gave it to her Lord to allow the divinity of the Son of God to come into humanity. But this humanity of Christ is also expressed in the fact that Mary creates around her son an ordinary Jewish family, guarantor of all the contributions of the Torah.

With John, we discovered a mother of astonishing audacity, capable of arousing the divine part of her son. Guardian of the "hour," Mary has the "intuition of the signs" that mark the ministry of Jesus. With the beloved disciple, she holds the remarkable privilege of making "the hour" come about in the course of time. Her symbolic motherhood has no end. Finally, Luke, in his Gospel, makes Mary the image of Israel who gives birth to the Messiah and, in Acts, he underlines that, through the action of the Spirit received at Pentecost, Mary is an accomplished disciple, on the same level as the Twelve.

All these achievements are camouflage for the thurifers of an evanescent role for Mary. However, she actively and convincingly demonstrates that Jesus is both man and God, and she accompanies the reader who enters into this mystery.

12

MARY, MODEL DISCIPLE

THROUGHOUT THE PREVIOUS chapters, we have commented on Mary's attitude and outlined the contours of her portrait. It remains to be seen whether she should be included among the disciples and, if so, to define what kind of disciple she is. To consider this new figure and determine how Mary encourages faith in her son, we will revisit from a new angle certain passages already discussed.

LISTEN, DISCERN, OBEY, WELCOME AS A REAL DISCIPLE

A disciple is one who follows Jesus Christ, both by faith and by works. Does Mary fit this definition? Three episodes show this unequivocally. These are the annunciation-Magnificat chapter in the Gospel of Luke (1:26–56), the scene at the cross in John (19:26–27), and the Upper Room–Pentecost episode in Acts (1:12–14; 2:1–4).

The annunciation depicts Mary as a figure of Israel who in all things "pleases the Lord." We have listed the various qualities that this implies.[1] The most decisive is listening, intelligent listening, as demonstrated by the question that Mary asks the angel. Then comes the ability to "move to action." Here, Mary's action is radical. Indeed, what decision is as binding as accepting the arrival of a child? By the "yes" that concludes her dialogue with the angel Gabriel, Mary reveals herself to be an authentic disciple. Then, through the Magnificat, Mary shows herself to be lucid about the abuse of power, and she exposes the social consequences to which following Christ leads.

What happens at the foot of the cross is also of decisive importance. We have shown that in welcoming "the mother," the beloved disciple receives into his home the entire messianic community that preceded him, of which Mary is the figure. And conversely, from that moment on, Mary is integrated into the believing community that surrounds Jesus. Thus, a woman of Israel allows disciples from all backgrounds, the "universal human," to join this assembly. This gift gives birth to an ecclesial community, perfectly mixed and familial. Mary is therefore a disciple of a very unique quality. Freed from her biological motherhood, she represents a welcome without any discrimination in the present and future life of this community.

Her discipleship is also confirmed at the very beginning of the Book of Acts when it is said that Mary and the group of apostles "were constantly devoting themselves to prayer" (1:14). Mary participates in person in this first believing assembly. Consequently, John and Luke agree on this fact: If the Mother becomes a disciple of Jesus, it is because she responded positively to Jesus's challenge—he who does the will of my Father is my mother, my brother, and so on. She is therefore part of his true family, in the broader sense that Jesus established, and thus shows that the future family of believers belongs to the Jewish tradition but also exceeds it. Jean-Pierre Lémonon shows that it is in this movement toward union that the Church is constituted.[2]

Luca Castiglioni then notes that from now on, in the Church, "no one must be elevated above the other, especially men over women."[3] Then he adds: "Mary and women, therefore, not only are an integral part of the praying community, but they receive the Spirit that empowers them to prophecy."[4] Thus Mary, the accomplished disciple, seems sent by Luke to announce the good news without the slightest mention of a subordination to the Twelve.

From these various episodes, it emerges that Mary, according to the biblical scholar André Wénin, "so close to the man Jesus through her motherhood, had to also live the paschal mystery of her Son to become a disciple in the Church. As a believer who receives the Holy Spirit, she traces a path for every Christian."[5]

It will come as no surprise to anyone that at the end of this book we reach the conclusion that not only is Mary a disciple, but she is the absolute model of one, for no other disciple has lived as close as she to the Son of God. Yet she is also a disciple in an unexpected way. When Luke mentions her without any particular regard at Pentecost, letting her blend into the group, does he not mean that she now becomes the most discreet? Consequently, any reader can announce the good news as she did.

THE POWER OF FAITH

Let us now seek to qualify what kind of disciple Mary is. In the abundant harvest of our investigation, several traits emerge.

The first aspect to remember is certainly her capacity to transgress, even at the cost of her own life. Indeed, the obligatory nature of the virginity of young girls is written in Jewish Law: "If...evidence of the young woman's virginity was not found,...the men of the town shall stone her to death, because she committed a disgraceful act in Israel by prostituting herself in her father's house" (Deut 22:20). Accepting a pregnancy incomprehensible in the eyes of the world, Mary is assumed to have lost her virginity. She conceives and practices a sort of "religious disobedience" toward the official prescriptions. The intelligence she demonstrates is based on an obedience superior to the laws of society, that which one owes to God, and she is justified in seeing in her response the hand of God, since the angel told her: "The Lord is with you" (Luke 1:28). It remains to dare. In this, she will join the example of the four women present in the genealogy of her son. Mary therefore knows how to obey, but in the primary sense of the original Latin term, *ob-audire*, to put one's ear before, while maintaining both freedom and reason.

The annunciation as well as the Magnificat also reveal Mary's charism of prophecy. Spokesperson for her son, as are the prophets, she does not hesitate to announce in this song the coming of salvation, the mercy of God, and the concern for the little ones, the humiliated, all those left behind by society. However, the final objective of the cause defended by Mary is not a simple desire for a reversal of power. Mary advocates the reconciliation of humanity with all those who compose it, small and great. She announces the rejection of the power that enslaves and subjugates people and deprives them of their own speech. The lesson, which the cross will push to its climax, is valid for everyone, yesterday as today. There is great courage in uttering the Magnificat, and prophets of all times have often paid for it with their lives. We still verify today the vigor and radicality of the moral injunction that Mary dared to take up for herself.

At Cana, her initiatives are those of an expert disciple. As a relative or friend of one of the spouses, she feels free to take the lead. As the first disciple in John's Gospel to speak in the name of Christ, once again she is daring.

However, she does not desire to impose herself in the life of her son, but to be available for what he is going to undertake. The same desire, no doubt, as that evoked in Luke when she answered the angel Gabriel: "Let it be with me according to your word!" (Luke 1:38). She perceived, in line with the prophet Isaiah, how to "make straight in the desert a highway for our God" (Isa 40:3). This places her at the service of her son, assuming a role that she has accepted and that is hers. During this wedding meal, the words she addresses to the servants also show her discernment and her prudence, that is to say, her understanding of situations and her accurate appreciation of the capacities of the one she invites to be daring.

Cana also highlights a very particular charism of Mary: her ability to anticipate, to move forward with audacity. It shows that the disciple may well be *following* Christ, but she is not an ordinary *follower*, but rather a pioneer. How far we are from the Mary promoted by the institution who withdraws from public affairs! If Mary shows a propensity to "meditate on all these things in her heart," this goes hand in hand with presence, action, and commitment in broad daylight. Mary proves that self-reflection, interiority, and public commitment are compatible and even, no doubt, indispensable to one another. In this, Mary is faithful to the Jewish tradition, and she contributes to making it also a Christian characteristic.

All these qualities recognized in Mary are based on the one principal foundation of discipleship: faith, the primary underpinning of all ministry. Mary believes what the angel Gabriel tells her. Even more, at Cana, she believes in her son. For her, faith is not a list of truths to be learned and recited. Believing is expressed in trust in others, in the conviction of a capacity that must be encouraged in oneself and toward others. Every disciple of Christ must be configured by trust, because there is no human growth without someone opposite you who looks at you and believes in you until "your hour" comes. Faith is also accompanied by education, by an awareness of the favorable moment, of the *kaïros*, an awareness that Jesus demonstrates. All life goes through these favorable moments, these decisive hours when one's deep identity is revealed, when a major decision is made. Mary makes this trust and this intuition of "the hour" a true ministry, adapted to ordinary daily relationships, which does not mean secondary as much as to exceptional circumstances.

John, by calling her "the mother," underlines that this role of disciple borrows from qualities of mothers that are often recognized in them and that have already been mentioned here under the term *Jewish mothers*. These are the joy of giving birth, the desire for the well-being and success of their offspring, the necessary renunciation of directing the life of another, the separation that is sometimes difficult to face. Added to this for Mary is the awareness of a sacrifice that pierces the heart. But we have also noted that at the cross, Mary goes beyond any gender assignment to become a universal model of the disciple, man or woman. Her charism of "giving birth" is extended to a motherhood of another type, a nongendered motherhood. This makes her an exceptional disciple.

All these observations reinforce the evidence that there are several characteristics of Mary portrayed in the Gospels in which Mary shines and which can benefit a life of faith. The first arises from the errors of history concerning her. As we have repeated, Mary is fully human. Consequently, seeking to make her a goddess is a serious error. An interesting way to realize this is to be attentive to the works of art that present her. Those that show her alone raise questions, because they predispose the viewer to this adoration that we have denounced. It is better to favor those where she is with others because Mary is never alone in the Gospels. She is always "in the company" of her husband, her cousin Elizabeth, her son, the shepherds, the Magi, her friends from Cana, or the beloved disciple. She is "one among others," within a community that she does not seek to flee and with which she remains united.

It seems important to us that Christians announce the Gospel with Mary, starting from her acquiescence to an ordinary humanity—earthy, humble, caring, capable, without unnecessary brilliance, risking transgression, and having a quiet audacity. Indirectly, her "yes" to herself and to what God can do with her questions the refusal of the human condition that lies dormant in most people, this very common desire for omnipotence, and sometimes a pressing need always to be protected, to have intercession as if one needed a safe conduct to heaven. Mary invites us to refuse all these escape routes and to humble ourselves. In short, she is a precious help for those who want to work on themselves.

Mary, by accepting her humanity, is, for Christianity, an essential asset in its proclamation of salvation. It is fortunate that she is neither Wonder Woman nor the Queen of Heaven of the land of Canaan against whom Jeremiah fought: "The women knead dough, to make cakes for the queen of heaven" (Jer 7:18). For salvation does not come from a desperate effort toward excess, but from a humanity that assumes itself.

A second characteristic flows from the first. If Mary is a disciple of Christ, it is because she teaches that he is coming. The "kerygma of Mary," the central announcement of her faith, is to have brought Christ into the world and therefore to invite everyone to do the same: "May Christ be born in your hearts as he was born in my womb."

Throughout history, the image of God's birth within the human race has been proposed particularly to religious men and women, ascetics, and contemplatives. But why would it be reserved for them? Mary is not a nun; she does not live withdrawn from the world. She goes to see her cousin, she raises her child, she goes to a wedding....Bringing Christ into the world and inviting others, saying that salvation has come near, is the goal of every life of faith. The mission of each Christian is fulfilled with this proclamation. We have amply shown that it is intended for all, women and men, even if this may seem, at first glance, disturbing to the latter. In order to feel comfortable with this, men must rediscover the poetry of the prophets who reach the universal without being paralyzed by gender.

Many situations in life are births that can take Mary as an example. Parents, educators, spiritual guides, caregivers, and artists have experienced this. In front of their students, many have accompanied births like Mary did at Cana. But God also invites Godself into families, into assemblies, into liberation struggles, into the contemplation of nature and the cosmos. God gives birth through conversion, forgiveness, the outstretched hand, the reconciliation of humanity with itself.

Relying on Mary, believers are responsible for relaying the good news, that is, to remind us that the world may be "modern," but it is not abandoned; it is still *gifted with God*, as Mary was. Mary's message is contained in these two invitations: to love who we are and to acquiesce to the coming of God. This message is available to whoever wants to seize it, well beyond Christian spheres. In our secularized world, Mary not only remains a disciple, but she encounters new causes that place her at the rank of universal disciple. Beyond labels, she speaks of the vocation of humanity: to refuse to be closed in on oneself, to know how to welcome the unexpected, that which is greater than oneself, to discern the divine in all things, to give birth in one's womb to the One who can reconcile humanity with itself and with the planet. For all currents of spirituality that are searching, the figure of Mary is precious and stimulating.

Mary is this accomplished disciple, the one we need today. We have amply recalled her gifts. She is capable of transgressions, of carrying the word of her son; she is gifted with prophecy, with the charism of anticipation that allows her to open doors rather than blindly following cruel prescriptions that discriminate against women, and she is capable of absolute trust in others. As we have recalled several times, she fulfills God's creation because she is the "help matched to the other." Beyond the charisms which are specific to her, she takes up the major announcement of the ministry of Jesus, that humanity must leave no one on its margins.

Let us admit that behaving like Mary is not as simple as the Gospel accounts would have us believe. How can we distinguish a call from the Spirit from a simple rebellion against the law? How can we trust without sometimes risking death? We can make mistakes, stray into silliness, or even harm the ones we wish to help. Anticipating another can be only a screen for establishing a hold over others. What defenses can we put up against these risks that punctuate every existence? Finally, how can we learn what she had to learn to become capable of saying "yes"? Perhaps we must give up trying to imitate her, in order to first enjoy the formidable dynamism that emerges from her life. To soak up her docility to the Spirit, her finesse, her vivacity. Then, to let ourselves be taught by such an accomplished life, to maintain a sustained companionship with her. Finally, thanks to this friendship that spans the ages, to try to be ourselves, always wary of the noise of the world, the complaints, and the human expectations, to give ourselves the freedom to create.

13

MARY, OUR SISTER

Mary, freed from pietistic inflations, political manipulations, and silent weakness. Mary brand new. Mary as the evangelists have portrayed her—an elder who supports the faith in its momentum toward Christ. Through deconstruction and investigation, a new portrait emerges from the rubble of the counterfeit image. Let us look one last time at who Mary is not.

No, Mary is not a "showpiece" who submits to the authority of the angel, nor a naïve ingénue who takes refuge in silence. If she "meditates on all things in her heart," she is not afraid to speak, and she even dares to intervene firmly.

No, Mary is not the model of the suffering mother, even if her son is the victim of abominable injustice. Never in the Gospels do we see her cry. Her suffering, if we can imagine it, is not reported, because Mary is not reduced to her pain.

No, Mary is not "the Holy Virgin," as if this qualifier were her identity. Apart from the indecency of naming women according to their gynecological condition. Do we call Jesus "virgin"? The term is improper. Yes, Mary is a virgin, but she is like all the young girls of her time in Israel. And according to the scriptures, her virginity speaks of waiting on God. She is absorbed in the wedding that, for Mary, occurs at the birth of the child-Messiah. What should be called "the virginal conception of Jesus" has a precise justification. It speaks of the power of God and Mary's readiness to accept God's Word. It places the emphasis on Jesus, not on the physical state of his mother. It can be understood literally, or symbolically in the manner of the prophets. However, there has been in the Church an *abuse of virginity* since the end of Antiquity. Until when will it continue? Not only is it wrong to continue today to call Mary "the Virgin," but it is even worse to give women the virginity of Mary as a model. All life choices are respectable, but linking physical virginity and knowledge of God is wrong. In no case can the virginity of Mary be used to justify physical virginity, because one does not conflate term-by-term a biological fact with a spiritual state. These are two levels that each have their own logic and are not interpreted by each other. We who have often spoken about Mary to audiences of women have each time noted the immense liberation that these few reminders have brought them. This model of virginity as a horizon of faith, underpinned by an injunction to purity, has done them unimaginable harm. It has reinforced in them anxiety, shame, guilt, malaise, and the feeling of servitude. "How to kill Jesus?"[1] asked an inspired Dominican recently in a book on abuse. How to kill Mary? That has been demonstrated for a long time.

However, virginity remains a spiritual reality that has value. It speaks of distance from idols, sometimes so prevalent in today's consumeristic world, of inner availability, indispensable for welcoming Christ within oneself, but only on the absolute condition that it be an invitation made to every human being.

No, Mary is not this absent, disembodied form, this ephemerality that Christian commentators have made of her by severing her from her sexual life for the rest of her days. Moreover, the episode of the woman with the issue of blood (Matt 9:20–22) clearly shows Jesus's concern to give back to every woman the possibility of a normal sexual life. Why have we not taken Jesus seriously? Not only is this obstinate desire of the Church to disincarnate Mary something monstrous because of the intensity of the hold that the institution has exercised over women, but we have long recalled that it is a major theological fault.

No, Mary is not the model of "the woman," or even "of" women. Women are incapable of assuming the double contradictory injunction to be mother and virgin at the same time. Furthermore, the characters of the Gospels are not defined by their gender qualities. Peter is no more a model reserved for men than Mary Magdalene is for women. How, in the twenty-first century, can the Church still advocate through the voice of its popes such a regression?

No, Mary is not a coredemptrix or mediatrix. Redemption, salvation, come from Christ alone. The Second Vatican Council firmly recalled this.[2]

From these ruins, another silhouette emerges whose outline is now clear in our minds. Mary is much more than we knew. Mary is the one who dares. She is sufficiently confident in God to contravene a law that would not smooth the paths of the Lord. In order to welcome within herself the unheard-of God, she assumes a transgression that is barely imaginable for us modern people. She goes beyond a taboo of her time. Worse still, at a time when life without the group was inconceivable, she puts herself outside the law. Before her son, who died as an outcast, Mary his mother dared to exclude herself. Do we often recall this in an institution that places obedience at the top of its virtues?

However, Mary is so confident in God that she meets God's messenger. But how did she recognize him? Did he come in a furtive thought, in a stubborn dissatisfaction, in an irresistible overflow of the heart? No one knows. But this ignorance is the reader's opportunity. It is up to each one to open our door to the angel...

And Mary said yes. She would carry, in her body, the good news of salvation. Not only in her spirit, but in her own body, her innermost being, her "garden," as the mystics and poets have said. She experienced daily the total humanity and the real divinity of her son. This adventure, assumed and lived, unfolded in a covenant. In Mary, the ancient covenant of Sinai is prolonged, knotted in the depths of the flesh. Mary weaves the First Testament with the New.

Mary has a certain affinity with the Spirit who is at her side, intimate with her, covering her thoughts, her words, her gestures. Mary is the one inspired by God, the one who leads to Christ by the certainty of her faith. Whoever believes, wants to believe, or does not know how to believe can find in her a precious help.

Is Mary a feminist? She probably never had to ask herself this question, which would be an anachronism to her. In Israel, the question of ontological inferiority did not arise. The God of the Bible created man and woman in God's image, equal from the clay, both endowed with the breath of the Spirit. Certainly, as in all ancient societies, life was strictly codified between feminine obligations and masculine duties. The Church, which has learned to discard outdated rites and codes when it found them inconvenient, still does not apply the full equality affirmed in the scriptures between men and women. It is far from having truly valued the action of Mary freeing herself from the social constraint linked to virginity that was so pervasive at that time. Mary went beyond it. In a certain way, she even freed humanity from it well before the movements for female emancipation. Let us salute the relevance and timeliness of her words uttered two thousand years ago! Mary tells whoever wants to hear her that a woman's body cannot be enslaved to any law, to any social constraint, nor to any man, even a fiancé, but that it remains free, for the intimate and indisputable choice that the subject makes of it. "My body is mine," she said, well before #MeToo. As stipulated in the World Health Organization's current reproductive rights statement,[3] "Free disposal of one's body" is a freedom that Mary lived. With her magnificent affirmation, Mary anticipated the developments of our modern societies. Without banners or slogans, she deploys her militancy in a simple acquiescence to the God "of her fathers." But in so doing, she demonstrates that this God frees humans from fathers who, sometimes, can be abusive. Her elder sister in the faith, the "chaste Suzanne," had already learned this to her detriment when she opposed two old men, judges recognized in the city and yet abusers. For all those young women who, even today, risk death at the hands of fathers or brothers who make their daughter's or sister's body a power struggle, Mary is the ultimate figure of courage. At the risk of her life, she said no to the social codes that "for the honor of the fathers" imposed virginity on young women. Under her liberating "godmotherhood," feminists of all religions have a true ally. It is up to them to draw inspiration from the work of liberation that Mary launched and that she illustrates so well. If the Church had not been blinded for centuries by male domination, it would have advocated the liberation of women's bodies under the banner of Mary, as it did in the first centuries, according to its first intuition, and it would undoubtedly be better off today.

Mary, daughter of Abraham, follower of a God who never ceases to educate God's people to a difficult freedom, is a free woman for a God who makes people free. The freedom with which she makes her decisions is remarkable. Freedom in relation to "what will people say," freedom in the face of the unknown to which her yes exposed her. Freedom of the children of God who move forward serenely in their choices.

Mary frees herself from the social roles that are linked to the condition of motherhood. She achieves the feat, exceptional for the time and still difficult today, of having had another life afterward. After the passion, having become again a disciple like the others, in tandem with the beloved disciple, "sent" like him, both apostles if there are any, Mary participates in the community of those who follow Christ. Yet this is hardly noticed by the Catholic Church. We see more of the opposite: Women are first and foremost the wives of "someone" and the mothers of "someone." Also, more than statues crowned with flowers, more than honeyed speeches, and more than praises launched into the azure of the sky, the faithful expect the Church, in the name of Mary, to entrust to women the legitimate responsibilities to which scripture obliges them because it is the very will of the Creator.

In the end, we ask Mary a long-standing question: How did she know that Jesus was the Christ, the one sent by God? She knows this from her daily association with the man of the Beatitudes. We know neither the pitfalls nor the passions of this companionship. They belong only to her. We can envy her, but we cannot take it away from her. For that reason alone, Mary cannot be imitated.

But how could she have understood a speech so far removed from the logic of the world? Certainly, the prophets taught her the basics. We could bet that the essential understanding came from that unique moment when, discovering the fruit of her womb, a weak and marvelous newborn, she "wrapped him...and laid him in a manger," understanding that he was "her Savior." Yet, she only saw a child whom she would have to take care of day and night....There, it seems to us, is the mystery into which she invites the reader to enter. The mystery of a weak God with whom the Creator's instruction is fulfilled, which we have recalled many times: that the other be "the helper." Mary illustrates this with the most convincing example, that of a totally dependent newborn. But two thousand years after Mary gave birth, her plea in favor of a weak God is still overridden by the fury of the world, which prefers to create a conquering God, in accordance with its expectations and dreams, an ideal and distant God that one would hope would "restore the kingdom to Israel" (Act 1:6). But this God is only the dream weapon of an all-too-human will to power. Mary, for her part, opens other paths that find their apotheosis in the sign of the cross. In Mary, seen from this new angle, we already experience what Jürgen Moltmann states: "It is only by giving up himself to open himself to what is foreign, unknown and other, that the human being can become himself," before adding: "Only he who finds the courage to be other than others can ultimately be there for the other."[4] This courage is that of being oneself, unique as the Christian message says. This is what Mary has illustrated.

All these qualities that we recognize in Mary make her both unique and contemporary. Her faith, her dynamism, her freedom, her radicalism, her feminism before its time, her theological accuracy reach out to us.

At a time when Catholic patriarchy is being contested and biblical fraternity is being rediscovered, it is useful to recall that for a father of the Church of the fourth century, Mary was a sister.[5] A sister? That seems so new in the Catholic world! And yet, what freshness, what novelty, what richness, what a future!

NOTES

CHAPTER 1

1. "Lobotomize" literally means to perform a surgical procedure consisting of cutting certain nerve fibers inside the brain. It is used here in a figurative sense: to make stupid, to be amputated of a part of oneself and one's faculties.

2. The Latin version does not mention Adam's name: "O certe necessárium Adae peccátum, quod Christi morte deletum est! O felix culpa, quae talem ac tantum méruit habére Redemptórem!" But the new liturgical translation according to the *Roman Missal* (3rd edition, 2021, 211) says: "O truly necessary sin of Adam, destroyed completely by the Death of Christ! O happy fault that earned so great, so glorious a Redeemer!"

3. Irenaeus of Lyons, *Against Heresies: Denunciation and Refutation of Gnosis with a Lying Name*, III, 22, trans. Adelin Rousseau (Cerf, 2001), 386.

4. Cf. Paul Beauchamp, *L'un et l'autre Testament. Accomplir les Écritures* (Grasset, 1990), 153.

5. This is how Lytta Basset understands it in *Guérir du malheur* (Albin Michel/Labor et Fides, 1999), 266, pointing out the insistence on the fact that Eve gives birth to "sons."

6. Beauchamp, *L'un et l'autre Testament,* 154.

7. Work by the painter Masolino da Panicale, Brancacci Chapel, Church of Santa Maria del Carmine, Florence, ca. 1524.

8. The Hebrew verb used in this verse is *shouwph*, which has only three occurrences in the Bible: here in Genesis 3:15; "he who in the whirlwind crushes me," in Job 9:17; and "let darkness swallow me up" in Psalm 139:11.

9. Gen 3:15, in the Bible of the French rabbinate; "this one will bruise your head and you will bruise her heel," in *TOB*.

10. Elizabeth A. Johnson, *Dieu au-delà du masculin et du féminin. Celui / Celle qui est*, trans. Pierrot Lambert (Cerf, 1999), 59–60.

11. Essentialist feminism considers that a person's sex determines their gender. Furthermore, their essence precedes their existence and makes them dependent on determinisms that affect certain behaviors. In this sense, men run the city and women "take care" of the private sphere. Few people in the West, outside of certain religious movements, adhere to this idea.

12. The term *dignity* is used thirteen times in the first seven paragraphs of *Mulieris Dignitatem*.

13. Cf. John Paul II, *Letter to Women*, June 29, 1995, 12: "It is in fact especially by giving herself to others in everyday life that woman realizes the profound vocation of her life, she who, perhaps even more than man, sees man, because she sees him with her heart."

14. Patrick Snyder, *La femme selon Jean-Paul II. Lecture des fondements anthropologiques et théologiques et des applications pratiques de son enseignement* (Fides, 1999).

15. John Paul II, *Letter to Women*, 3.

16. John Paul II, *Letter to Women*, 8.

17. Snyder, *La femme selon Jean-Paul II*, 131.

18. 1975–1995.

19. Anne-Marie Pelletier, et al., *Se réformer ou mourir. Sept théologiennes prennent la parole* (Salvator, 2023), 70.

20. Gauthier Vaillant, "Les cinq phrases marquantes du pape François sur les femmes," in *La Croix*, May 25, 2015.

21. Rita Amabili, "La fraise théologienne ou analyse du regard pontifical sur la moitié de l'humanité," October 29, 2015, femmes-ministeres.lautreparole.org.

22. Pope Francis, "Address at the Marian Vigil in Trujillo," in *Salt and Light*, January 21, 2018.

CHAPTER 2

1. "Never enough."

2. Michel Psellos quoted in Enzo Bianchi, "Prier Marie selon les Écritures," in *Biblia*, Hors-série-Revues (Cerf, 2006), 45.

3. Dominique Cerbelaud, *Marie. Un parcours dogmatique* (Cerf, 2003), 214.

4. Yves Congar, *Journal d'un théologien. 1946–1956* (Cerf, 2000), 296.

5. Study commission mandated by l'Arche International, *Emprise et abus. Enquête sur Thomas Philippe et Jean Vanier,* report of January 30, 2023.

6. Xavier Moutard, *Contes et légendes du Lauzet. En Briançonnais* (Les Alpes de Lumière, 2002), 134.

7. Laure Charpentier, *La Macarena. La Vierge qui pleure et qui console* (Grancher, 2013).

8. C. Blanchard and I. Seguin, song "*Regarde l'étoile,*" L'Emmanuel, after Bernard of Clairvaux.

9. Louis-Marie Grignion de Montfort, *Traité de la vraie dévotion à la Sainte Vierge* (Seuil, 1996).

10. Alphonse de Liguori, *Les gloires de Marie* (Saint-Paul, 1998).

11. Jean-François Villepelée, *L'Immaculée révèle l'Esprit Saint. Entretiens spirituels du père Kolbe* (Lethielleux, 1974).

12. Leonardo Boff, *O rosto matemo de Deus. Ensato interdisciplinar sobre o feminino e suas formas religiosas,* 11th ed. (Vozes, 2012).

13. Cerbelaud, *Marie*, 203.

14. The *ecumene* is the set of inhabited areas.

15. Pius IX, *Ineffabilis Deus*, On the Immaculate Conception, December 8, 1954, https://www.papalencyclicals.net/pius09/p9ineff.htm.

16. Pius XII, *Munificentissimus Deus*, Defining the Dogma of the Assumption, November 1, 1950, https://www.vatican.va/content/pius-xii/en/apost_constitutions/documents/hf_p-xii_apc_19501101_munificentissimus-deus.html, 44.

17. *Documentation catholique* 2113 (April 2, 1995), 693.

18. Joseph Ratzinger, *Voici quel est notre Dieu* (Plon / Mame, 2001), 215–16.

19. A dogmatic council establishes dogmas while Vatican II is a "pastoral" council, that is, intended for a better proclamation of the Gospel.

20. Uta Ranke-Heinemann, *Des eunuques pour le royaume des cieux. L'Église catholique et la sexualité,* trans. Monique Thiollet (Robert Laffont, 1990).

21. International Theological Commission, *On the Interpretation of Dogmas,* 1989.

22. Despite a justification from the magisterium that says it consulted Catholics through the nunciatures, thus having honored the *sensus fidei,* the "sense of faith" of the faithful.

23. Walter Kasper, *Dogme et Évangile* (Casterman, 1967), 28.

24. Pope Francis, *Un temps pour changer. Conversations avec Austen Ivereigh* (Flammarion, 2020), 89.

CHAPTER 3

1. See chapter 2, "Four Dogmas of Mary."
2. *TOB*, note p. 2098.
3. *TOB*, note p. 653.
4. To read more on this subject see Peter Brown, *Le Renoncement à la chair. Virginité, célibat et continence dans le christianisme primitif* (Gallimard, 1995).
5. Sandrick Le Maguer, *Portrait d'Israël en jeune fille. Genèse de Marie* (Gallimard, 2008), 193; cf. Amos 5:1–4.
6. Micheline Gagnon, "La virginité dans la Bible hébraïque et le judaïsme," *L'autre Parole* 125 (2010).
7. Ignatius of Antioch, *Lettre aux Éphésiens* (19:1), trans. Pierre-Thomas Camelot (Cerf, 1968), 87–89.
8. Apocryphal texts are those that are not included in the official canon of the Church.
9. Athanasius of Alexandria, *Letter to the Virgins.*
10. Ephrem of Syria, *Hymn of B. Maria,* 10, 19.
11. Gregory of Nazianzus, *Oratio* 38, 1, PG 36, 313 A.
12. Origen, *In Cantica,* 2.
13. *Protoevangelium of James,* chapters 17–20.
14. Donna Singles, *L'homme debout. Le credo de saint Irénée* (Cerf, 2008), 52.
15. Bernard Sesboüé, *Pédagogie du Christ. Éléments de christologie fondamentale* (Cerf, 1994), 203.
16. Sesboüé, *Pédagogie du Christ*, 228.
17. Joseph Ratzinger, *Foi chrétienne hier et aujourd'hui* (Mame, 1969), 192.
18. Christian Duquoc, *La femme, le clerc et le laïc* (Labor et Fides, 1989), 32.
19. Cf. Paul Beauchamp, *L'un et l'autre Testament. Accomplir les Écritures* (Grasset, 1990).
20. Augustine of Hippo, *Du mariage et de la concupiscence. Lettre au comte Valère* (Blanche de Peuterey, 2018).
21. Jean-Yves Loude, *Le chemin des vierges enceintes. Une autre voie pour Compostelle* (Chandeigne, 2022).

22. Quoted by Uta Ranke-Heinemann, *Des eunuques pour le royaume des cieux. L'Église catholique et la sexualité,* trans. Monique Thiollet (Robert Laffont, 1990), 32.

23. According to Atton, Bishop of Vercelli, the ban dates back to the Council of Laodicea (canon 11), around 364. But there are many later declarations that renew it. Cf. Georgio Otranto, "The Priesthood of Women in Christian Antiquity," on the website womenpriests.org.

24. This anthropological construction will probably be abolished if, according to what Henri Atlan announced in *L'Utérus artificiel,* La Librairie du XXIe Siècle (Seuil, 2005), we manage to create human beings outside of a maternal uterus, definitively disconnecting the feminine from the gift of life. It is likely, then, that all gender barriers will be abolished.

CHAPTER 4

1. Ariane Buisset, *Les Religions face aux femmes* (Accarias l'Originel, 2008), 63.

2. Georgette Blaquière, *La Grâce d'être femme* (1981) (Saint-Paul, 1984), 52–53.

3. Schalom Ben-Chorin, *Un regard juif sur la mère de Jésus* (Desclée de Brouwer, 2001).

4. Charles Péguy, *Le Porche du mystère de la deuxième vertu* (1911) (Gallimard, 1986): "She who is infinitely queen / Because she is the humblest of creatures / Because she was a poor woman, a miserable woman, a poor Jewess from Judea. / To her who is infinitely far / Because she is infinitely near."

5. See chapter 6, "Four Subversive Women."

CHAPTER 5

1. Cf. Sylvaine Landrivon, *Faites-les taire. Judith, un enseignement subversif* (Olivétan, 2014).

2. Pontifical Biblical Commission, *L'interprétation de la Bible dans l'Église* (Cerf, 1994).

3. Cf. Sylvaine Landrivon, *La femme remodelée. Centrer la grâce d'être femme sur la maternité: choix de Dieu ou des hommes?* (Cerf, 2016).

4. Including Jean-Louis Ska and Marie de Mérode.

5. André Wénin, *Pas seulement de pain...Violence et alliance dans la Bible*, Lectio divina (Cerf, 1998), 48.

6. Cf. Elizabeth Moltmann-Wendel, in Elizabeth and Jürgen Moltmann, *Dieu. Homme et femme,* trans. Marcelline Brun-Reyniers (Cerf, 1984).

7. Georgette Blaquière, *Oser vivre l'amour* (1997) (Éditions des Béatitudes, 2005), 34–35.

8. Wénin, *Pas seulement de pain,* 52.

9. For the sake of convenience, we will call him Abraham even when he has not yet acquired that name. The same goes for Sarai, who is called Sarah.

10. Jean-Pierre Lémonon, *Pour lire l'Évangile selon saint Jean* (Cerf, 2020), 534.

11. Cf. chapter 3, "Virginity in the Ancient World."

12. This is the meaning that can be given here to the term *chofèt.*

13. Lappidoth is the husband of Deborah. His name in Hebrew means "torches" and, indeed, he seems be a well-enlightened man since he accepts being the spouse of a woman invested with great responsibilities.

14. Cf. Irmtraud Fischer, *Des femmes aux prises avec Dieu* (Cerf, 2008); *Des femmes messagères de Dieu* (Cerf, 2009).

15. Cf. Philippe Abadie, *La reine masquée. Lecture du livre d'Esther* (Profac, 2011); "Judith et Esther," in *Biblia* 76 (February 2009).

CHAPTER 6

1. See chapter 5, under the section "Is the Biblical Universe Hostile to Women?"

CHAPTER 7

1. Cf. Anne Soupa, *Judas. Le coupable idéal* (Albin Michel, 2018).

2. *The Annunciation* (1528), Civic Museum Villa Colloredo Mels, Recanati, Italy.

3. All these qualities of the people are present in Deuteronomy.

4. Sandrick Le Maguer, *Portrait d'Israël en jeune fille. Genèse de Marie* (Gallimard, 2008), 193.

5. See chapter 3, under "Virginity in the Ancient World."

6. Luca Castiglioni, *Filles et fils de Dieu. Égalité baptismale et différence sexuelle*, Cogitatio fidei (Cerf, 2020), 468.

7. Zachariah loses the power of speech until the moment of naming his son.

8. See chapter 5, under the heading "Other Women, Often Prophetesses."

9. It is the pious fiction by which the Book of Deuteronomy or "second Law" was inserted into the Torah.

CHAPTER 8

1. Eliminated in 1975.

2. Dominique Cerbelaud, *Marie. Un parcours dogmatique* (Cerf, 2003), 219.

3. Jürgen Moltmann, *L'Église dans la force de l'Esprit. Une contribution à l'ecclésiologie moderne*, trans. Robert Givord (Cerf, 1980), 111.

4. Gustavo Gutiérrez, *Théologie de la libération. Perspectives*, trans. François Malley (Lumen Vitae, 1974), 298.

5. September 13, 2013.

6. Jürgen Moltmann, *Le Dieu crucifié. La croix du Christ, fondement et critique de la théologie chrétienne,* Cogitatio fidei (Cerf, 1974), 30–31.

7. Maria Teresa Porcile Santiso (1943–2001) was a Roman Catholic lay theologian from Uruguay, specializing in biblical studies, teaching philosophy in Montevideo, involved in ecumenical and interreligious initiatives with the Pontifical Council for Christian Unity and the World Council of Churches.

8. Maria Teresa Porcile Santiso, *La femme, espace de salut. Mission de la femme dans l'Église. Une perspective anthropologique* (Cerf, 1999), 368–69.

CHAPTER 9

1. The Spirit of God "came down" on Samson (cf. Judg 14:6), on David (cf. 1 Sam 16), and on Isaiah (cf. Isa 16:1).

2. Cf. Dan 12:10–12: "He said: 'Go, Daniel; these words are closed and sealed until the time of the End. Many will be washed, made white and purified; the wicked will do wickedly, the wicked will not understand; the learned will understand. From the time when the daily sacrifice is abolished and the abomination of desolation is set up.'"

3. Etty Hillesum, *Une vie bouleversée. Journal 1941–1943* (1985), *followed by Lettres de Westerbork*, trans. Philippe Noble (Seuil, 1995), 166.

4. See chapter 4 under "A Motherhood with Symbolic Connotations Too."

5. Saint Ignatius of Loyola, *Exercices spirituels,* Points-Sagesses (Seuil, 1982), 113.

6. Augustine of Hippo, *The Confessions,* trans. Joseph Trabucco (Flammarion, 1964), book 10, chap. 27.

7. Tertullian, *The Flesh of Christ,* Christian Sources 216 (Cerf, 1975), vol. I, vol. IV, chap. 1, 221–27.

8. Jean-Paul Sartre, "Bariona" (1940), in *Théâtre complet,* Library of the Pleiades 512 (Gallimard, 2005), 1164. See table, scene 3.

CHAPTER 10

1. Charles Perrot, *Marie de Nazareth au regard des chrétiens du premier siècle*, Lectio divina 255 (Cerf, 2013), 145–49.

2. See "What Is Mary Called in the New Testament" below.

3. This is the case the first time Luke has to name her. Then he calls her "Mary" or "his mother" (of the child).

4. See chapter 3 under "Brothers and Sisters of Jesus."

CHAPTER 11

1. Irenaeus of Lyons, *Against Heresies,* III. 16, 7, p. 353.

2. Note that the only other allusion to *womb* (here with *kolpos* but later, in a more prosaic way with the term *koilia*) in the mouth of Jesus is found in John 7:37–38 when he refers to Scripture to say: "On the last day of the festival, the great day, while Jesus was standing there, he cried out, "Let anyone who is thirsty come to me, and

let the one who believes in me drink. As the scripture has said, 'Out of the believer's belly shall flow rivers of living water.'"

3. The Jerusalem Bible, the Segond Bible, the Bayard Bible, the Crampon Bible, the Luther Bible, while in a note, the *TOB*, alone, mentions that it is about "the mother."

4. Jean-Pierre Lémonon, *Pour lire l'Évangile selon saint Jean* (Cerf, 2020), 534.

5. Isaiah 66:7–8: "Before she was in labor / she gave birth; / before her pain came upon her / she delivered a son. / Who has heard of such a thing? / Who has seen such things? / Shall a land be born in one day? / Shall a nation be delivered in one moment? / Yet as soon as Zion was in labor / she delivered her children.

6. John the Baptist is killed by Herod (cf. Mark 6:17–29).

7. This persecution can be seen when the Magi visit Herod and understand, through a dream, that they should not return to tell him where the child Jesus is (cf. Matt 2:12). It is evident during the massacre of the Holy Innocents (cf. Matt 2:16–17).

8. Max Thurian, *Marie, mère du Seigneur. Figure de l'Église*, Living Faith 61 (Les Presses de Taizé, 1968).

9. See "Apocalypse, Eschatology" above.

10. John the Baptist embodies the spirit of the First Testament prophets and fulfills their announcements, serving as a theological and spiritual link between the two testaments. We understand it in Malachi 3:1: "See, I am sending my messenger to prepare the way before me." This verse is often interpreted by Christians as foreshadowing John the Baptist. Isaiah 40:3: "A voice cries out: 'In the wilderness prepare the way of the Lord, make straight in the desert a highway for our God.'" This passage is explicitly applied to John the Baptist in the Gospels (see Luke 3:4; Matthew 3:3; Mark 1:3).

11. "All these were constantly devoting themselves to prayer, together with certain women, including Mary the mother of Jesus, as well as his brothers."

12. For further study of these different christological approaches, see in particular the interviews of Bernard Sesboüé with Marc Leboucher, *La théologie au XXe siècle et l'avenir de la foi* (Desclée de Brouwer, 2007).

13. Bernard Sesboüé, *Jésus-Christ dans la tradition de l'Église* (1982) (Desclée de Brouwer, 2000), 23–24.

CHAPTER 12

1. See chapter 7.

2. Jean-Pierre Lémonon, *L'Epître aux Galates* (Cerf, 2008).

3. Luca Castiglioni, *Filles et fils de Dieu. Égalité baptismale et différence sexuelle*, Cogitatio fidei (Cerf, 2020), 472.

4. Castiglioni, *Filles et fils de Dieu*, 473.

5. André Wénin, Camille Focant, and Sylvie Germain, *Vives femmes de la Bible* (Lessius, 2007), 138–39.

CHAPTER 13

1. Philippe Lefebvre, *Comment tuer Jésus? Abus, violences et emprises dans la Bible*, LeXio (Cerf, 2023).

2. *Lumen Gentium* 62: "The Blessed Virgin is invoked by the Church under the titles of Advocate, Auxiliatrix, Adjutrix, and Mediatrix. This, however, is to be so understood that it neither takes away from nor adds anything to the dignity and efficaciousness of Christ, the one Mediator. For no creature could ever be counted as equal with the Incarnate Word and Redeemer."

3. "[Reproductive rights] are based on the recognition of the fundamental right of all couples and individuals to decide freely and responsibly on the number and spacing of their children....This right is also based on the right of all people to make reproductive decisions free from discrimination, coercion, or violence as expressed in human rights documents." World Health Organization, 2009.

4. Jürgen Moltmann, *Le Dieu crucifié. La croix du Christ, fondement et critique de la théologie chrétienne* (1974), trans. Bernard Fraigneau-Julien, Cogitatio fidei (Cerf, 1978), 23.

5. Athanasius of Alexandria, *Letter to Epictetus*, 4, 5–7, PG t. 26, col. 1061 B, in "Prier Marie avec les Écritures," *Biblia*, special issue 1:40.

BIBLIOGRAPHY

Beauchamp, Paul. *Parler d'Écritures saintes*. Seuil, 1987.

Beauchamp, Paul. *L'un et l'autre Testament. Accomplir les Écritures*. Grasset, 1990.

Castiglioni, Luca. *Filles et fils de Dieu. Égalité baptismale et différence sexuelle*. Cerf, 2020.

Cerbelaud, Dominique. *Marie. Un parcours dogmatique*. Cerf, 2003.

Congar, Yves. *Journal d'un théologien. 1946–1956*. Cerf, 2000.

Groupe des Dombes. *Marie dans le dessein de Dieu et la communion des saints*. Bayard / Centurion, 1999.

Johnson, Elizabeth A. *Dieu au-delà du masculin et du féminin. Celui / Celle qui est*. Translated by Pierrot Lambert. Cerf, 1999.

Porcile Santiso, Maria Teresa. *La femme, espace de salut. Mission de la femme dans l'Église. Une perspective anthropologique*. Cerf, 1999.

Quesnel, Michel, and Philippe Gruson. *La Bible et sa culture*. Desclée de Brouwer, 2000.

Ranke-Heinemann, Uta. *Des eunuques pour le royaume des cieux. L'Église catholique et la sexualité*. Translated by Monique Thiollet. Robert Laffont, 1990.

Snyder, Patrick. *La femme selon Jean-Paul II. Lecture des fondements anthropologiques et théologiques et des applications pratiques de son enseignement*. Fides, 1999.

Wénin, André. *Pas seulement de pain...Violence et alliance dans la Bible*. Cerf, 1999.

www.ingramcontent.com/pod-product-compliance
Lightning Source LLC
LaVergne TN
LVHW050642100826
845148LV00011B/1949

* 9 7 8 0 8 0 9 1 5 7 9 9 0 *